Praise for Anne Appl

TWILIGHT OF DEMOCRACY

"*Twilight of Democracy* offers many lessons on the long-standing struggle between democracy and dictatorship. But perhaps the most important is how fragile democracy is: Its survival depends on choices made every day by elites and ordinary people." —*The Washington Post*

"One of the many welcome aspects to [this] book is its acknowledgment that democracy, like any other form of government, is not forever. It cannot be a machine that would go of itself; it is a machine that, instead, goes only as long as its users care for it."
—*Los Angeles Review of Books*

"There is no single reason that liberal democracy is in such a precarious state, Applebaum notes. Crisp, elegant prose." —*The Christian Science Monitor*

"Thought-provoking and gracefully written."
—*The American Interest*

"If anyone is well placed to write about the global rise of authoritarian regimes and their polarization of society, it is Applebaum." —*The Arts Fuse*

"An illuminating political memoir about the breakup of the political tribe that won the Cold War."
—*Literary Review* (London)

"Engrossing. . . . This is a political book; it is also intensely personal, and the more powerful for it."
—*The Guardian*

"[Applebaum] deploys the roles of both historian and hostess to impressive effect. . . . [A] penetrating work of ethnography, a novel study of the intellectual tribe to which the author belongs."
—*The Sunday Times* (London)

"The risk of twilight of our western democratic model, the uncertainty of what may follow—a brighter dawn or a darker night—require that all warnings be urgently considered. This book demands such consideration."
—*The Irish Times*

"Critically important for its muscular, oppositionist attack on the new right from within conservative ranks—and for the well-documented warning it embodies. [Applebaum's] views are especially welcome because she is a deliberate thinker and astute observer rather than just the latest pundit or politico. . . . A knowledgeable, rational, necessarily dark take on dark realities."
—*Kirkus Reviews* (starred review)

Anne Applebaum

TWILIGHT OF DEMOCRACY

Anne Applebaum's 2018 *Atlantic* article "A Warning from Europe" inspired this book and was a finalist for a National Magazine Award. After seventeen years as a columnist at *The Washington Post*, Applebaum became a staff writer at *The Atlantic* in 2020. She is the author of three critically acclaimed and award-winning histories of the Soviet Union: *Red Famine*, *Iron Curtain*, and *Gulag*, winner of the Pulitzer Prize.

www.anneapplebaum.com

ALSO BY ANNE APPLEBAUM

Red Famine: Stalin's War on Ukraine

Iron Curtain: The Crushing of Eastern Europe, 1944–1956

Gulag: A History

Between East and West: Across the Borderlands of Europe

TWILIGHT *of* DEMOCRACY

TWILIGHT *of* DEMOCRACY

The Seductive Lure of Authoritarianism

Anne Applebaum

ANCHOR BOOKS

A Division of Penguin Random House LLC

New York

FIRST ANCHOR BOOKS EDITION, JUNE 2021

Copyright © 2020 by Anne Applebaum

All rights reserved. Published in the United States by Anchor
Books, a division of Penguin Random House LLC, New York.
Originally published in hardcover in the United States by Doubleday,
a division of Penguin Random House LLC, New York, in 2020.

Anchor Books and colophon are registered trademarks
of Penguin Random House LLC.

Portions of this book originally appeared in the following
publications: "A Warning from Europe: The Worst Is Yet
to Come" (October 2018) and "The People in Charge See an
Opportunity" (March 23, 2020) first published in *The Atlantic.*
"Want to Build a Far-Right Movement? Spain's Vox Party Shows
How" first published in *The Washington Post* (May 2, 2019).

The Library of Congress has cataloged the Doubleday edition as follows:
Name: Applebaum, Anne, author.
Title: Twilight of democracy : the seductive lure
of authoritarianism / Anne Applebaum.
Description: First edition. | New York : Doubleday, 2020. |
Includes bibliographical references.
Identifiers: LCCN 2020012450
Subjects: LCSH: Authoritarianism. | Democracy. | Nationalist
parties. | One-party systems. | World politics—21st century.
Classification: LCC JC480 .A67 2020 | DDC 321.9— dc23
LC record available at https://lccn.loc.gov/2020012450

Anchor Books Trade Paperback ISBN: 978-1-9848-9950-7
eBook ISBN: 978-0-385-54581-5

Author photograph courtesy of the author
Book design by Michael Collica

www.anchorbooks.com

Printed in the United States of America
10   9   8   7   6   5   4

Our age is indeed the age of the intellectual organization of political hatreds. It will be one of its chief claims to notice in the moral history of humanity.

—Julien Benda, *La trahison des clercs,* 1927

We must accept the fact that this kind of rebellion against modernity lies latent in Western society . . . its confused, fantastic program, its irrational and unpolitical rhetoric, embodies aspirations just as genuine . . . as the aspirations in other and more familiar movements of reform.

—Fritz Stern, *The Politics of Cultural Despair,* 1961

Contents

I   *New Year's Eve*   1

II   *How Demagogues Win*   22

III   *The Future of Nostalgia*   55

IV   *Cascades of Falsehood*   105

V   *Prairie Fire*   142

VI   *The Unending of History*   172

   Acknowledgments   191

   Notes   193

TWILIGHT *of* DEMOCRACY

New Year's Eve

On December 31, 1999, we threw a party. It was the end of one millennium and the start of a new one, and people very much wanted to celebrate, preferably somewhere exotic. Our party fulfilled that criterion. We held it at Chobielin, a small manor house in northwest Poland that my husband and his parents had purchased a decade earlier—for the price of the bricks—when it was a mildewed, uninhabitable ruin, unrenovated since the previous occupants fled the Red Army in 1945. We had restored the house, or most of it, though very slowly. It was not exactly finished in 1999, but it did have a new roof as well as a large, freshly painted, and completely unfurnished salon, perfect for a party.

The guests were various: journalist friends from London and Moscow, a few junior diplomats based in Warsaw, two friends who flew over from New York. But most of them were Poles, friends of ours and colleagues of my husband, Radek Sikorski, who was then a deputy foreign minister in a center-right Polish government. There were local friends, some of Radek's school friends, and a large group of cousins. A handful of youngish Polish journalists came too—none then particularly famous—along with a few civil servants and one or two very junior members of the government.

You could have lumped the majority of us, roughly, in the general category of what Poles call the right—the conservatives, the anti-Communists. But at that moment in history, you might also have called most of us liberals. Free-market liberals, classical liberals, maybe Thatcherites. Even those who might have been less definite about the economics did believe in democracy, in the rule of law, in checks and balances, and in a Poland that was a member of NATO and on its way to joining the European Union (EU), a Poland that was an integrated part of modern Europe. In the 1990s, that was what being "on the right" meant.

As parties go, it was a little scrappy. There was no such thing as catering in rural Poland in the 1990s, so my mother-in-law and I made vats of beef stew and roasted beets. There were no hotels, either, so our hundred-odd guests stayed in local farmhouses or with friends in the nearby town. I kept a list of who was staying where, but a couple of people still wound up sleeping on the floor in the basement. Late in the evening we set off fireworks—cheap ones, made in China, which had just become widely available and were probably extremely dangerous.

The music—on cassette tapes, made in an era before

Spotify—created the only serious cultural divide of the evening: the songs that my American friends remembered from college were not the same as the songs that the Poles remembered from college, so it was hard to get everybody to dance at the same time. At one point I went upstairs, learned that Boris Yeltsin had resigned, wrote a brief column for a British newspaper, then went back downstairs and had another glass of wine. At about three in the morning, one of the wackier Polish guests pulled a small pistol out of her handbag and shot blanks into the air out of sheer exuberance.

It was that kind of party. It lasted all night, continued into "brunch" the following afternoon, and was infused with the optimism I remember from that time. We had rebuilt our ruined house. Our friends were rebuilding the country. I have a particularly clear memory of a walk in the snow—maybe it was the day before the party, maybe the day after—with a bilingual group, everybody chattering at once, English and Polish mingling and echoing through the birch forest. At that moment, when Poland was on the cusp of joining the West, it felt as if we were all on the same team. We agreed about democracy, about the road to prosperity, about the way things were going.

That moment has passed. Nearly two decades later, I would now cross the street to avoid some of the people who were at my New Year's Eve party. They, in turn, would not only refuse to enter my house, they would be embarrassed to admit they had ever been there. In fact, about half the people who were at that party would no longer speak to the other half. The estrangements are political, not personal. Poland is now one of the most polarized societies in Europe, and we have found ourselves on opposite sides of a profound divide, one that runs through not only what used to be the Polish right but also the old Hungarian right, the Spanish right, the French right, the Italian right, and, with some differences, the British right and the American right, too.

Some of my New Year's Eve guests—along with me and my husband—continued to support the pro-European, pro-rule-of-law, pro-market center right. We remained in political parties that aligned, more or less, with European Christian Democrats, with the liberal parties of France and the Netherlands, and with the Republican Party of John McCain. Some of my guests consider themselves center-left. But others wound up in a different place. They now support a nativist party called Law and Justice—a party that has moved dramatically away from the positions it held when it first briefly ran the government, from 2005 to 2007, and when it occupied the presidency (not the same thing in Poland) from 2005 to 2010.

In the years it was out of power, the leaders of Law and Justice and many of its supporters and promoters slowly came to embrace a different set of ideas, not just xenophobic and paranoid but openly authoritarian. To be fair to the electorate, not everybody could see this: Law and Justice ran a very moderate campaign in 2015 against a center-right party that had been in power for eight years—my husband was a member of that government, though he resigned before the election—and was in the final year headed by a weak and unimpressive prime minister. Understandably, Poles wanted a change.

But after Law and Justice won a slim majority in 2015, its radicalism immediately became clear. The new government violated the constitution by improperly appointing new judges to the constitutional court. Later, it used an equally unconstitutional playbook in an attempt to pack the Polish Supreme Court and wrote a law designed to punish judges whose verdicts contradicted government policy. Law and Justice took over the state public broadcaster—also in violation of the constitution—firing popular presenters and experienced reporters. Their replacements, recruited from the far-right extremes of the online media, began running straightforward ruling-party propaganda, sprinkled with easily disprovable lies, at taxpayers' expense.

State institutions were another target. Once in power, Law and Justice sacked thousands of civil servants, replacing them with party hacks, or else cousins and other relatives of party hacks. They fired army generals who had years of expensive training in Western academies. They fired diplomats with experience and linguistic skills. One by one, they wrecked cultural institutions too. The National Museum lost its excellent acting director, an internationally respected curator. He was replaced with an unknown academic, with no prior museum experience, whose first major decision was to dismantle the museum's exhibition of modern and contemporary art. A year later he would resign, leaving the museum in chaos. The director of the Museum of the History of Polish Jews—an institution unique in Europe, opened with great fanfare only a few years earlier—was suspended from his job with no explanation, horrifying the museum's international supporters and funders. Those stories were echoed by thousands of others that didn't make headlines. A friend of ours lost her job in another state institution, for example, after she had completed too many projects too quickly. Her new and unqualified director seemed to perceive her as a threat.

There was very little pretense about any of this. The point of all of these changes was not to make government run better. The point was to make the government more partisan, the courts more pliable, more beholden to the party. Or maybe we should call it, as we once did, the Party.

They had no mandate to do this: Law and Justice was elected with a percentage of the vote that allowed them to rule but not to change the constitution. And so, in order to justify breaking the law, the party stopped using ordinary political arguments, and began identifying existential enemies instead. Some were old and familiar. After two decades of profound Polish-Jewish conversations and reconciliation—after thousands of books, films, and conferences, after the construction of that spectacular museum—the government earned

international notoriety by adopting a law curtailing public debate about the Holocaust. Although they eventually
changed the law under American pressure, it enjoyed
broad support among the party's ideological base—the
journalists, writers, and thinkers, including some of my
party guests, who now say they believe that anti-Polish
forces are plotting to blame Poland instead of Germany
for Auschwitz. Later, the party also involved itself in a
pointless spat with the Israeli government, an argument
that seemed designed to appeal both to Law and Justice's
angry, nationalist voters in Poland and Benjamin Netanyahu's angry, nationalist voters in Israel.

Some of the enemies were new. After a brief period
of attacking Islamic immigrants—difficult, in a country
with almost no Islamic immigrants at all—the party
focused its ire on homosexuals. A national weekly, *Gazeta
Polska*—a couple of whose most prominent journalists
were at my New Year's Eve party—printed "LGBT Free
Zone" stickers for its readers to put on their doors and
windows. On the eve of another parliamentary election
in October 2019, state television showed a documentary
called *Invasion,* describing the secret "LGBT" plan to
undermine Poland. The Polish Catholic church, once a
neutral institution and an apolitical symbol of national
unity, began promoting similar themes. The current
archbishop of Krakow, a title previously held by Pope
John Paul II, gave a sermon describing homosexuals as
a rainbow-colored "plague" that had replaced the "red
plague" of Communism. His sermon was applauded by

the Polish government and then removed from YouTube by online moderators, on the grounds that it constituted hate speech.

This sequence of events now makes it difficult for me and some of my New Year's guests to speak about anything at all. I have not, for example, had a single conversation with Ania Bielecka, formerly one of my closest friends—the godmother of one of my children—since a hysterical phone call in April 2010, a couple of days after a plane carrying the then president crashed near Smolensk, in Russia, about which more in a moment. Bielecka is an architect whose other friends include, or anyway used to include, some of the best-known artists of her generation; she also enjoys, or used to enjoy, contemporary art exhibitions, even traveling a few times to the Venice Biennale, just for fun. She once told me she enjoyed people watching at the Biennale—all of the arty ladies in their elaborate outfits—as much as the exhibitions. But in recent years she has grown close to Jarosław Kaczyński, the leader of Law and Justice and the late president's twin brother. She now regularly hosts lunches for Kaczyński at her apartment—she is a great cook—and discusses whom he should appoint to his cabinet. I am told that the culture minister, the author of the assault on Polish museums, was her suggestion. I tried to see her a couple of years ago in Warsaw, but she refused. "What would we talk about?" she texted me, and then went silent.

Another of my guests—the one who shot the pistol in

the air—eventually separated from her British husband. Her eccentricity has been transformed into something else, and she appears to spend her days as a full-time Internet troll, fanatically promoting a whole range of conspiracy theories, many of them virulently anti-Semitic. She tweets about Jewish responsibility for the Holocaust; she once posted an image of an English medieval painting depicting a boy supposedly crucified by Jews, with the commentary "And they were surprised that they were expelled," referring to the expulsion of the Jews from Britain in 1290. She follows and amplifies the leading lights of the American "alt-right," whose language she repeats and promotes.

A third guest, the journalist Anita Gargas, has spent the past decade investigating, over and over again, a set of conspiracy theories involving the death of the late president, Lech Kaczyński, in the Smolensk plane crash, each time postulating a different explanation. She's employed by *Gazeta Polska,* the weekly newspaper that distributed the antigay stickers. A fourth guest, Rafal Ziemkiewicz, has made a name for himself as an outspoken opponent of the international Jewish community. He refers to Jews as "scabby" and "greedy," calls Jewish organizations "blackmailers," and regrets his former support for Israel. The notoriety he gained from this language appears to have bolstered what had been his faltering career, and he now appears frequently on party-controlled state television.

I happen to know that some of these ex-friends are

estranged from their children because of their political views. In a couple of cases, the estrangement is profound. One of my former friends, though deeply committed to a political party with an openly homophobic agenda, has a gay son. But that too is typical—these divides run through families as well as groups of friends. We have a neighbor near Chobielin whose parents listen to a progovernment, Catholic-conspiratorial radio station called Radio Maryja. They repeat its mantras, make its enemies their enemies. "I've lost my mother," my neighbor told me. "She lives in another world."

To fully disclose all of my interests here, I should explain that some of this conspiratorial thinking is focused on me. My husband was the Polish defense minister for a year and a half, in a coalition government led by Law and Justice during its first, brief experience of power. Later, he broke with that party and was for seven years the foreign minister in another coalition government, this one led by the center-right party, Civic Platform. In 2019, he ran for the European Parliament and won a seat, though he is not currently part of the leadership of the political opposition.

I have lived in Poland on and off since 1988, with large chunks of time spent in London and Washington, writing history books and working as a journalist for British and American newspapers. That makes me an exotic political spouse by Polish standards, though until 2015 most people were curious about me rather than angry. I never experienced any direct anti-Semitism, never felt any hostility; when I published a Polish cookbook—intended, among other things, to overturn negative stereotypes about Poland outside the country—the reaction inside Poland, even among Polish chefs, was largely positive, if a little bemused. I also tried quite hard to stay out of politics, mostly avoiding Polish television except to speak about my books.

But after Law and Justice won, negative articles about the government began appearing abroad—and I was blamed. I was featured on the covers of two pro-regime magazines, *wSieci* and *Do Rzeczy* (former friends of ours work at both), as the clandestine Jewish coordinator of the international press and the secret director of its negative coverage of Poland; one of them invented details about my family in order to make it seem more sinister. Similar stories appeared on state television's evening news broadcast, along with another, wholly invented story about how the Law and Justice Party had gotten me fired from a job that I didn't have. Eventually they stopped writing about me: negative international press coverage of Poland finally grew much too widespread for a single person, even a single Jewish person, to coordinate all by herself, though naturally, the theme recurs on social media from time to time. During my husband's European election campaign, some of his team were asked more questions about me and my "anti-Polish activity" than about him. Whether I like it or not, I am part of this story.

When this all began, I felt a kind of déjà vu. I remembered reading a famous journal kept by the

Romanian writer Mihail Sebastian from 1935 to 1944. In it, he chronicled an even more extreme shift in his own country. Like me, Sebastian was Jewish, though not religious; like me, most of his friends were on the political right. In the journal, he described how, one by one, they were drawn to fascist ideology, like a flock of moths to an inescapable flame. He recounted the arrogance and confidence his friends acquired as they moved away from identifying themselves as Europeans—admirers of Proust, travelers to Paris—and instead began to call themselves blood-and-soil Romanians. He listened as they veered into conspiratorial thinking or became casually cruel.

People he had known for years insulted him to his face and then acted as if nothing had happened. "Is friendship possible," he wondered in 1937, "with people who have in common a whole series of alien ideas and feelings—so alien that I have only to walk in the door and they suddenly fall silent in shame and embarrassment?" In an autobiographical novel he wrote at the same time, the narrator offers friendship to an old acquaintance, from whom he is now divided by politics. "No, you're wrong," comes the response: "The pair of us can't be friends. Now or ever. Don't you get the smell of the land off me?"

Today is not 1937. Nevertheless, a parallel transformation is taking place in my own time, both among the thinkers, writers, journalists, and political activists in Poland, a country where I have lived for three decades, as well as in the rest of the societies we have come to call the West. Everywhere, this transformation is taking place without the excuse of an economic crisis of the kind Europe and North America suffered in the 1920s and 1930s. The recession of 2008–2009 was deep, but—at least until the coronavirus pandemic—growth had returned. The refugee crisis of 2015–2016 was a shock, but it has abated. By 2018, refugees from North Africa and the Middle East had mostly stopped coming to Europe, thanks to deals done with Turkey by the EU and its mainstream politicians.

In any case, the people I am writing about in this book were not affected by either of these crises. They are perhaps not all as successful as they would like to be, but they are not poor and rural. They have not lost their jobs to migrant workers. In Eastern Europe, they are not victims of the political transition since 1989, or of politics in any sense at all. In Western Europe, they are not part of an impoverished underclass, and they do not live in forgotten villages. In the United States, they do not live in communities ravaged by opioids, they do not spend much time in midwestern diners, and they do not, in fact, match any of the lazy stereotypes used to describe Trump voters at all—including some of the lazy stereotypes they have invented themselves. On the contrary, they have been educated at the best universities, they often speak foreign languages, they live in big cities—London, Washington, Warsaw, Madrid—and they travel abroad, just like Sebastian's friends in the 1930s.

What, then, has caused this transformation? Were

some of our friends always closet authoritarians? Or have the people with whom we clinked glasses in the first minutes of the new millennium somehow changed over the subsequent two decades?

There is no single explanation, and I will not offer either a grand theory or a universal solution. But there is a theme: Given the right conditions, any society can turn against democracy. Indeed, if history is anything to go by, all of our societies eventually will.

The ancient philosophers always had their doubts about democracy. Plato feared the "false and braggart words" of the demagogue, and suspected democracy might be nothing more than a staging point on the road to tyranny. Early American advocates of republican government also recognized the challenge that a corrupt leader could pose to democracy, and thought hard about creating the institutions that would resist one. The Constitutional Convention of 1787 created the electoral college as a means of ensuring that a man with what Alexander Hamilton called "talents for low intrigue, and the little arts of popularity" could never become president of the United States. Although it eventually became a rubber-stamp body with no power—and, more recently, a mechanism that gives outsize influence to small groups of voters in a few states—the electoral college was originally meant to be something quite different: it was designed as a kind of review board, a group of elite lawmakers and

men of property who would select the president, rejecting the people's choice if necessary, in order to avoid the
"excesses of democracy."

Hamilton was one of many in colonial America who
read over and over again the history of Greece and Rome,
trying to learn how to prevent a new democracy from
becoming a tyranny. In his old age, John Adams was
once again reading Cicero, the Roman statesman who
sought to halt the deterioration of the Roman Republic,
even quoting him in letters to Thomas Jefferson. They
wanted to build democracy in America on the basis of
rational debate, reason, and compromise. But they had
no illusions about human nature: They knew that men
could sometimes succumb to "passions," to use their old-
fashioned word. They knew that any political system
built on logic and rationality was always at risk from an
outburst of the irrational.

In modern times, their successors have searched to
define that irrationality and those "passions" further, and
to understand who might be drawn to a demagogue and
why. Hannah Arendt, the original philosopher of totalitarianism, identified an "authoritarian personality," a
radically lonely individual who "without any other social
ties to family, friends, comrades or even mere acquaintances, derives his sense of having a place in the world
only from his belonging to a movement, his membership
in the party." Theodor Adorno, one of a generation of
intellectuals who fled Nazi Germany for America, investigated that idea further. Influenced by Freud, Adorno

sought to find the source of the authoritarian personality in early childhood, perhaps even in repressed homosexuality.

More recently, Karen Stenner, a behavioral economist who began researching personality traits two decades ago, has argued that about a third of the population in any country has what she calls an authoritarian predisposition, a word that is more useful than *personality,* because it is less rigid. An authoritarian predisposition, one that favors homogeneity and order, can be present without necessarily manifesting itself; its opposite, a "libertarian" predisposition, one that favors diversity and difference, can be silently present too. Stenner's definition of *authoritarianism* isn't political, and it isn't the same thing as *conservatism.* Authoritarianism appeals, simply, to people who cannot tolerate complexity: there is nothing intrinsically "left-wing" or "right-wing" about this instinct at all. It is anti-pluralist. It is suspicious of people with different ideas. It is allergic to fierce debates. Whether those who have it ultimately derive their politics from Marxism or nationalism is irrelevant. It is a frame of mind, not a set of ideas.

But theorists often leave out another crucial element in the decline of democracy and the construction of autocracy. The mere existence of people who admire demagogues or feel more comfortable in dictatorships does not fully explain why demagogues win. The dictator wants to rule, but how does he reach that part of the public that feels the same? The illiberal politician wants to undermine courts in order to give himself more power, but how does he persuade voters to accept those changes? In ancient Rome, Caesar had sculptors make multiple versions of his image. No contemporary authoritarian can succeed without the modern equivalent: the writers, intellectuals, pamphleteers, bloggers, spin doctors, producers of television programs, and creators of memes who can sell his image to the public. Authoritarians need the people who will promote the riot or launch the coup. But they also need the people who can use sophisticated legal language, people who can argue that breaking the constitution or twisting the law is the right thing to do. They need people who will give voice to grievances, manipulate discontent, channel anger and fear, and imagine a different future. They need members of the intellectual and educated elite, in other words, who will help them launch a war on the rest of the intellectual and educated elite, even if that includes their university classmates, their colleagues, and their friends.

In his 1927 book *La trahison des clercs*—loosely translated as "The Treason of the Intellectuals" or sometimes "The Betrayal of the Intellectuals"—the French essayist Julien Benda observed and described the authoritarian elites of his time long before anyone else understood how important they were. Anticipating Arendt, his concern was not "authoritarian personalities" as such, but rather the particular people who supported the authoritarianism that he already saw taking both left- and right-wing forms all across Europe. He described both far-right and far-left ideologues who sought to promote either "class passion," in the form of Soviet Marxism, or "national passion," in the form of fascism, and accused them both of betraying the central task of the intellectual, the search for truth, in favor of particular political causes. Sarcastically, he called these fallen intellectuals *clercs* or "clerks," a word whose oldest meanings link it to "clergy." Ten years before Stalin's Great Terror and six years before Hitler came to power, Benda already feared that the writers, journalists, and essayists who had morphed into political entrepreneurs and propagandists would goad whole civilizations into acts of violence. And so it came to pass.

If it happens, the fall of liberal democracy in our own time will not look as it did in the 1920s or 1930s. But it will still require a new elite, a new generation of *clercs,* to bring it about. The collapse of an idea of the West, or of what is sometimes called "the Western liberal order," will need thinkers, intellectuals, journalists, bloggers, writers, and artists to undermine our current values, and then to imagine the new system to come. They may come from different places: in Benda's original definition, the *clercs* included ideologues of the right as well as the left. Both are still with us. An authoritarian sensibility is unquestionably present in a generation of far-left campus agitators who seek to dictate how professors can teach and what students can say. It is present in the instigators of

Twitter mobs who seek to take down public figures as well as ordinary people for violating unwritten speech codes. It was present among the intellectuals turned spin doctors of the British Labour Party who prevented any challenge to Jeremy Corbyn's leadership, even as it became clear that Corbyn's far-left agenda would be rejected by the country. It was present among the Labour activists who first denied and then downplayed the anti-Semitism that spread within the party too.

But although the cultural power of the authoritarian left is growing, the only modern *clercs* who have attained real *political* power in Western democracies—the only ones operating inside governments, participating in ruling coalitions, guiding important political parties— are members of movements that we are accustomed to calling the "right." They are, it is true, a specific kind of right, one that has little in common with most of the political movements that have been so described since the Second World War. British Tories, American Republicans, East European anti-Communists, German Christian Democrats, and French Gaullists all come from different traditions, but as a group they were, at least until recently, dedicated not just to representative democracy, but to religious tolerance, independent judiciaries, free press and speech, economic integration, international institutions, the transatlantic alliance, and a political idea of "the West."

By contrast, the new right does not want to conserve

or to preserve what exists at all. In continental Europe, the new right scorns Christian Democracy, which used its political base in the church to found and create the EU after the nightmare of the Second World War. In the United States and the United Kingdom, the new right has broken with the old-fashioned, Burkean small-*c* conservatism that is suspicious of rapid change in all its forms. Although they hate the phrase, the new right is more Bolshevik than Burkean: these are men and women who want to overthrow, bypass, or undermine existing institutions, to destroy what exists.

This book is about this new generation of *clercs* and the new reality they are creating, beginning with a few whom I know in Eastern Europe and then moving to the different but parallel story of Britain, another country where I have deep ties, and finishing with the United States, where I was born, with a few stops elsewhere. The people described range from nativist ideologues to high-minded political essayists; some of them write sophisticated books, others launch viral conspiracy theories. Some are genuinely motivated by the same fears, the same anger, and the same deep desire for unity that motivates their readers and followers. Some have been radicalized by angry encounters with the cultural left, or repulsed by the weakness of the liberal center. Some are cynical and instrumental, adopting radical or authoritarian language because it will bring them power or fame. Some are apocalyptic, convinced that their societies have failed and need to be reconstructed, whatever the result.

Some are deeply religious. Some enjoy chaos, or seek to promote chaos, as a prelude to imposing a new kind of order. All of them seek to redefine their nations, to rewrite social contracts, and, sometimes, to alter the rules of democracy so that they never lose power. Alexander Hamilton warned against them, Cicero fought against them. Some of them used to be my friends.

II

How Demagogues Win

MONARCHY, TYRANNY, OLIGARCHY, DEMOCRACY— all of these ways of organizing societies were familiar to Plato and Aristotle more than two thousand years ago. But the illiberal one-party state, now found all over the world—think of China, Venezuela, Zimbabwe—was first developed by Lenin, in Russia, starting in 1917. In the political science textbooks of the future, the Soviet Union's founder will surely be remembered not just for his Marxist beliefs, but as the inventor of this enduring form of political organization. It is the model that many of the world's autocrats use today.

Unlike Marxism, the illiberal one-party state is not a philosophy. It is a mechanism for holding power, and it functions happily alongside many ideologies. It works because it clearly defines who gets to be the elite—the political elite, the cultural elite, the financial elite. In the monarchies of prerevolutionary France and Russia, the right to rule was granted to the aristocracy, which defined itself by rigid codes of breeding and etiquette. In modern Western democracies, the right to rule is granted, at least in theory, by different forms of competition: campaigning and voting, meritocratic tests that determine access to higher education and the civil service, free markets. Old-fashioned social hierarchies are usually part of the mix, but in modern Britain, America, France, and, until recently, Poland, most assumed that democratic competition is the most just, and efficient, way to distribute power. The most appealing and competent politicians should rule. The institutions of the state—the judiciary, the civil service—should be occupied by qualified people. The contests between them should take place on an even playing field, to ensure a fair outcome.

Lenin's one-party state was based on different values. It overthrew the aristocratic order, but it did not put a competitive model in its place. The Bolshevik one-party state was not merely undemocratic; it was also anticompetitive and antimeritocratic. Places in universities, civil service jobs, and roles in government and industry did not go to the most industrious or the most capable: they went to the most loyal. Individuals advanced not because of talent or industry, but because they were willing to conform to the rules of the party. Though those rules were different at different times, they were consistent in certain ways. They usually excluded the former ruling elite and their children, as well as suspicious ethnic groups. They favored the children of the working class. Above all, they favored people who loudly professed belief in the party, who attended party meetings, who participated in public displays of enthusiasm. Unlike an ordinary oligarchy, the one-party state allows for upward mobility: true believers can advance—a prospect especially appealing to people whom the previous regime or society had not promoted. Arendt observed the attraction of authoritarianism to people who feel resentful or unsuccessful back in the 1940s, when she wrote that the worst kind of one-party state "invariably replaces all first-rate talents, regardless of their sympathies, with those crackpots and fools whose lack of intelligence and creativity is still the best guarantee of their loyalty."

Lenin's disdain for the idea of a neutral state, for apolitical civil servants and for any notion of an objective media, was an important part of his one-party system too. He wrote that freedom of the press "is a deception." He mocked freedom of assembly as a "hollow phrase." As for parliamentary democracy itself, that was no more than "a machine for the suppression of the working class." In the Bolshevik imagination, the press could be free, and public institutions could be fair, only once they were controlled by the working class—via the party.

The far left's mockery of the competitive institutions of "bourgeois democracy" and capitalism, its cynicism about the possibility of any objectivity in the media, the civil service, or the judiciary, has long had a right-wing version too. Hitler's Germany is the example usually given. But there are many others, from Franco's Spain to Pinochet's Chile. Apartheid South Africa was a de facto one-party state that corrupted its press and its judiciary to exclude blacks from political life and promote the interests of Afrikaners, white South Africans descended mainly from Dutch settlers, who were not succeeding in the capitalist economy created by the British Empire.

It's true that there were other parties in apartheid South Africa. But a one-party state is not necessarily a state with no opposition parties at all. Although Lenin's Communist Party and Hitler's Nazi Party arrested and murdered their opponents, there are plenty of examples of one-party states, even quite vicious one-party states, that permitted some limited opposition, if only for show. Between 1945 and 1989, many of the communist parties of Eastern Europe allowed opponents—peasants' parties, pseudo–Christian Democrats, or in the case of Poland, a small Catholic party—to play roles in the state, in the rigged "parliaments," or in public life. In recent decades, there have been many examples, from Ben Ali's Tunisia to Hugo Chavez's Venezuela, of de facto one-party states that controlled state institutions and limited freedom of association and speech, but allowed a token opposition to exist, so long as that opposition didn't actually threaten the ruling party.

This form of soft dictatorship does not require mass violence to stay in power. Instead, it relies upon a cadre of elites to run the bureaucracy, the state media, the courts, and, in some places, state companies. These modern-day *clercs* understand their role, which is to defend the leaders, however dishonest their statements, however great their corruption, and however disastrous their impact on ordinary people and institutions. In exchange, they know that they will be rewarded and advanced. Close associates of the party leader can become very wealthy, receiving lucrative contracts or seats on state company boards without having to compete for them. Others can count on government salaries as well as protection from accusations of corruption or incompetence. However badly they perform, they will not lose their jobs.

Around the world, there are many versions of the illiberal one-party state, from Putin's Russia to Duterte's Philippines. In Europe, there are many would-be illiberal parties, some of which have been part of ruling coalitions, for example in Italy and Austria. But as I write this, only two such illiberal parties have monopolies on power: Law and Justice, in Poland, and Viktor Orbán's Fidesz party, in Hungary. Both have made major steps toward the destruction of independent institutions, and both have showered benefits on their members as a result. Not only did Law and Justice change the civil service law, making it easier to fire professionals and hire party hacks, it also fired heads of Polish state companies. People with experience running large companies were replaced by party members, as well as their friends and relatives. Typical is Janina Goss, an avid maker of jams and preserves and an old friend of Kaczyński's from whom the prime minister once borrowed a large sum of money, to pay for a medical treatment for his mother. She had held some low-level party jobs before—but now she was named to the board of directors of Polska Grupa Energetyczna, the largest power company in Poland, an employer of forty thousand people. In Hungary, Viktor Orbán's son-in-law is a similarly wealthy, privileged figure. He was accused of defrauding the EU, but no investigation was ever completed. The case against him was dropped by the Hungarian state.

You can call this sort of thing by many names: nepotism, state capture, corruption. But if you so choose, you can also describe it in positive terms: it represents the end of the hateful notions of meritocracy, political competition, and the free market, principles that, by definition, have never benefited the less successful. A rigged and uncompetitive system sounds bad if you want to live in a society run by the talented. But if that isn't your primary interest, what's wrong with it?

If you believe, as many of my old friends now believe, that Poland will be better off if it is ruled by people who loudly proclaim a certain kind of patriotism, people who are loyal to the party leader, people who are, echoing the words of Kaczyński himself, a "better sort of Pole"—then a one-party state is actually *more* fair than a competitive democracy. Why should different parties be allowed to compete on an even playing field if only one of them deserves to rule? Why should businesses be allowed to compete in a free market if only some of them are loyal to the party and therefore truly deserving of wealth?

This impulse is reinforced, in Poland as well as in Hungary and many other formerly Communist countries, by the widespread feeling that the rules of competition are flawed because the reforms of the 1990s—when mass privatization and the imposition of free-market rules transformed the economies—allowed too many former Communists to recycle their political power into economic power. Both Orbán and Kaczyński frequently describe their opponents as "Communists," and even win over foreign admirers for doing so. In Orbán's case, his primary opponents, at least in the earlier part of his career, really were former Communists, renamed as "socialists," so this description had some power.

But in both countries this appeal to "anti-Communism," which felt so important a quarter century ago, seems thin and superficial now. Since at least 2005, Poland has been led solely by presidents and prime ministers whose political biographies began in the anti-Communist Solidarity movement. Kaczyński's primary rivals are in the liberal center right, not on the left. There is no powerful ex-Communist business monopoly in Poland either—at least not at the national level, where plenty of people have made money without special political connections. Indeed, the most prominent ex-Communist in Polish politics right now is Stanisław Piotrowicz, a former Communist prosecutor in the martial law era, now Law and Justice's nominee to the Constitutional Court. He is, unsurprisingly, a great enemy of judicial independence. Orbán regularly employs former

Communists in high posts too. The "anti-Communism" of both governments is another form of hypocrisy.

Nevertheless, grim warnings about the influence of "Communism" retain an appeal for the right-wing ideologues of my generation. For some of them, it seems to explain their personal failures, or just their bad luck. Not everybody who was a dissident in the 1970s got to become a prime minister, or a bestselling writer, or a respected public intellectual after 1989—and for many this is a source of burning resentment. If you are someone who believes that you deserve to rule, then your motivation to attack the elite, pack the courts, and warp the press to achieve your ambitions is strong. Resentment, envy, and above all the belief that the "system" is unfair—not just to the country, but to you—these are important sentiments among the nativist ideologues of the Polish right, so much so that it is not easy to pick apart their personal and political motives.

Certainly that's what I learned from the story of Jacek Kurski, the director of Polish state television and the chief ideologist of the would-be one-party state. He started out in the same place, at the same time, as his brother, Jarosław Kurski, who edits the largest and most influential liberal Polish newspaper. Born in the same family, they believe in two very different ideas of Poland. They are two sides of the same Polish coin.

—

To understand the Kurski brothers, it's important to understand where they came from: the port city of Gdańsk, on the Baltic Sea, where shipyard cranes loom like giant storks over old Hanseatic street facades. The Kurskis came of age there in the early 1980s, when Gdańsk was both the hub of anti-Communist activity in Poland and a shabby backwater, a place where intrigue and boredom were measured out in equal doses.

At that particular moment, in that particular place, the Kurski family stood out. Anna Kurska was a lawyer and a judge, active in the Solidarity trade union, the main opposition organization at the time. At home, their door was always open; all day long, people would stop by, hoping to discuss some urgent legal matter, maybe get some advice. Then they would stay, chat, drink tea, smoke, drink tea again, and chat some more. Nobody phoned up in advance, in 1980s Gdańsk. People didn't have telephones, or if they did they didn't trust them not to be bugged.

Anna's sons became activists too. Senator Bogdan Borusewicz, one of the most important underground trade-union activists from the time, told me that their school was widely known to be *zrewoltowane*—rebellious, in revolt against the Communist system. Jarosław represented his class in the school "parliament," an opposition initiative; he was also part of a group that read Polish conservative philosophy and literature. Jacek, slightly younger, was less interested in the intellectual battle against Communism. He thought of himself rather as an activist and a radical. After martial law was declared in 1981, ending the brief period of Solidarity's legal existence, both brothers went to marches, shouted slogans, waved banners. Both worked first on the illegal school newspaper and then on *Solidarność,* the illegal opposition newspaper of Solidarity.

In October 1989, Jarosław went to work as the press secretary to Lech Wałęsa, the leader of Solidarity, who, after the election of Poland's first non-Communist government, felt out of sorts and ignored; in the chaos created by revolutionary economic reforms and rapid political change, there was no obvious role for him. Eventually, at the end of 1990, Wałęsa ran for president and won, partly by galvanizing people who already resented the compromises that had accompanied the negotiated collapse of Communism in Poland, most notably the decision not to jail former Communists. The experience made Jarosław realize that he didn't like politics, especially not the politics of resentment: "I saw what doing politics was really about . . . awful intrigues, searching for dirt, smear campaigns."

That was also his first encounter with Kaczyński, later the founder of Law and Justice, who Jarosław told me was "a master of all that. In his political thinking, there is no such thing as an accident. . . . If something happened, it was the machination of an outsider. *Conspiracy* is his favorite word." (Unlike Jarosław, Jacek would not speak with me. A mutual friend—we have several— gave me his private cell phone number; I texted, and then called a couple of times and left messages. I called again and someone cackled when I stated my name, repeated it loudly, and said, "Of course, of course"—naturally the chairman of Polish television would return my call. But he never did.)

Eventually Jarosław quit and joined *Gazeta Wyborcza,* a newspaper founded at the time of Poland's first partially free elections, in 1989. In the new Poland, he could help build something, create a free press, he told me, and that was enough for him. Jacek went in precisely the opposite direction. "You are an idiot," he told his brother when he learned Jarosław had quit working for Wałęsa. Although he was still in high school, Jacek was already interested in a political career himself, and even suggested that he take over his brother's job, on the grounds that no one would notice: "There was Jarek, now there's Jacek. Who can tell the difference?"

Jacek was—in his brother's description—always "fascinated" by the Kaczyński brothers, who were plotters, schemers, inventors of conspiracies right from the beginning. At the same time, he was not particularly interested in the trappings of Polish conservatism, in the books or the debates that had captivated his brother. A friend of them both told me she didn't think Jacek had any real political philosophy at all. "Is he a conservative? I don't think so, at least not in the strict definition of conservatism. He's a person who wants to be on top." And from the late 1980s onward, that was where he aimed to be.

The sort of emotions that don't usually get much

attention from great political theorists played a big role in what happened next. Jacek Kurski is not a radically lonely conformist of the kind described by Hannah Arendt, and he does not incarnate the banality of evil; he is no bureaucrat following orders. He has never said anything thoughtful or interesting on the subject of democracy, a political system that he neither supports nor denounces. He is not an ideologue or a true believer; he is a man who wants the power and fame that he feels he has been unjustly denied. To understand Jacek, you need to look beyond political science textbooks and study, instead, literary antiheroes. You could look at Shakespeare's Iago, who manipulated Othello by playing on his insecurity and his jealousy. You could study Stendhal's Julien Sorel, who murdered his mistress when she stood in the way of his personal advancement.

Resentment, revenge, and envy, not radical loneliness, form the backdrop to what happened next. Jacek eventually turned against Wałęsa, perhaps because Wałęsa didn't give him the job he thought he deserved. He married and divorced; he sued his brother's newspaper several times, and the newspaper sued him back. He coauthored a fiery book and made a conspiratorial film about the secret forces lined up against the Polish right. Both projects gave him a certain cachet among the group who felt, like him, unfairly excluded from power in the first twenty-five years of post-Communist Poland.

Jacek was also a member, at different times, of different parties or factions, sometimes quite marginal and sometimes more centrist. He was a member of parliament for one term, where he made no mark. He was a member of the European Parliament, for one term, and made no mark there either. He came to specialize in so-called "black" PR. Famously, he helped torpedo the presidential campaign of Donald Tusk (who eventually became prime minister of Poland, and then president of the European Council) in part by spreading the rumor that Tusk had a grandfather who had voluntarily joined the Wehrmacht, the Nazi army. Asked about this invention, Jacek reportedly told a small group of journalists that of course it wasn't true, but *"ciemny lud to kupi"*—which, roughly translated, means "The ignorant peasants will buy it." Bogdan Borusewicz, the legendary Solidarity leader, describes him as "without scruples."

But although he spent years in public life, Jacek did not win the popular acclaim he thought that he, as a former teenage Solidarity activist, was entitled to. And this, his brother believes, was a huge disappointment: "All of his life, he believed that he is owed a great career . . . that he will be prime minister, that he is predestined to do something great. Yet fate dictated that he failed over and over again. . . . He concluded that this was a great injustice." By contrast Jarosław was successful, a member of the establishment, the editor of what was arguably the country's most important newspaper.

In 2015, Kaczyński plucked Jacek out of the relative obscurity of fringe politics and made him the director of state television. And this, it would seem, was Jacek's chance to exorcise his frustrations. Try to imagine what would happen to the BBC if it were taken over by the conspiracy website InfoWars: that will give you a rough idea of what happened to Telewizja Polska, Poland's public broadcaster, the operator of several radio and television channels and still the main source of news for a large part of the population. Jacek's destruction of state media was unconstitutional—after 1989, state television was supposed to become public television, politically neutral like the BBC. But it was nevertheless very thorough, the work of a man driven by a need for revenge.

The best-known journalists were fired and replaced by people who had previously worked for the far-right press, on the fringes of public life. Very quickly, news broadcasts ceased to make any pretense of objectivity or neutrality. Instead, they produced twisted news reports and carried out extensive vendettas against people and organizations whom the ruling party didn't like. As it turned out, these vendettas were not just ugly, they were lethal. For months on end they ran a vicious, repetitive campaign against the popular mayor of Gdańsk, Paweł Adamowicz, accusing him of everything from corruption to treason. And someone was listening: On January 13, 2019, a recently released criminal, who had been watching state television in prison, leapt onto a stage at the climactic moment of a charity concert and plunged a knife into Adamowicz's chest. The mayor died the next day.

Neither Kurski nor Kaczyński ever acknowledged the

role that the channel had played in radicalizing the murderer. On the contrary: Instead of apologizing, Telewizja Polska turned its venom on others. Among them was the new mayor of Gdańsk, Alexandra Dulkiewicz, who now needs a bodyguard. The mayor of Poznań, along with several other mayors, has had death threats as well. The taboo against political violence has been broken in Poland, and no one is certain who might be the next victim.

Still there has been no retreat, no acknowledgment that the constant drumbeat of hatred might inspire another assassination. The channel does not pay lip service to fairness. It does not employ any neutral commentators. On the contrary, it celebrates its own ability to manipulate reality. At one point in 2018, the station showed a clip from a press conference; the then leader of the opposition party, Grzegorz Schetyna, was asked what his party achieved during its eight years in government, from 2007 to 2015. The clip shows Schetyna pausing and frowning; the video slows down and then ends. It's as if he had nothing to say.

In reality, Schetyna spoke for several minutes about the mass construction of roads, investments in the countryside, and advances in foreign policy. But this manipulated clip—one example of many—was deemed such a success that for several days, it remained pinned to the top of Telewizja Polska's Twitter feed. Under Law and Justice, state television doesn't just produce regime propaganda; it draws attention to the fact that it is doing so.

It doesn't just twist and contort information, it glories in deceit.

Jacek—deprived of respect for so many years—finally got his revenge. Even after he formally stepped aside as television director—for some inside his party he began to go too far—he remains right where he thinks he should be: at the center of attention, the radical throwing Molotov cocktails into the crowd. His frustration, born of his inability to advance in a political system that favored rationality and competence, has now been overcome. The illiberal one-party state suits him perfectly; the uglier it becomes, the more fear he will inspire, the more power he will have. Communism isn't available anymore as an enemy to fight. But new enemies can be found. His victory over them will make him even greater.

From Orwell to Koestler, the European writers of the twentieth century were obsessed with the idea of the Big Lie, the vast ideological constructs that were Communism and fascism. The posters demanding fealty to the Party or the Leader, the Brownshirts and Blackshirts marching in formation, the torch-lit parades, the terror police—these forced demonstrations of support for Big Lies were so absurd and inhuman that they required prolonged violence to impose and the threat of violence to maintain. They required forced education, total control of all culture, the politicization of journalism, sports, literature, and the arts.

By contrast, the polarizing political movements of twenty-first-century Europe demand much less of their followers. They do not espouse a full-blown ideology, and thus they don't require violence or terror police. They want their *clercs* to defend them, but they do not force them to proclaim that black is white, that war is peace, and that state farms have achieved 1,000 percent of their planned production. Most of them don't deploy propaganda that conflicts with everyday reality. And yet all of them depend, if not on a Big Lie, then on what the historian Timothy Snyder once told me should be called the Medium-Size Lie. To put it differently, all of them encourage their followers to engage, at least part of the time, with an alternative reality. Sometimes that alternative reality has developed organically; more often, it's been carefully formulated, with the help of modern marketing techniques, audience segmentation, and social-media campaigns.

Americans are of course familiar with the ways a lie can increase polarization and inflame xenophobia. Long before he ran for president, Donald Trump entered American politics promoting birtherism, the false premise that President Barack Obama was not born in America—a conspiracy theory whose power was seriously underestimated at the time. But in at least two European countries, Poland and Hungary, we now have examples of what happens when a Medium-Size Lie— a conspiracy theory—is propagated first by a political party as the central plank of its election campaign, and then by a ruling party, with the full force of a modern, centralized state apparatus behind it.

In Hungary, the lie is unoriginal: It is the belief, now promoted by the Russian government and many others, in the superhuman powers of George Soros, the Hungarian Jewish billionaire who is supposedly plotting to destroy Hungary through the deliberate importation of migrants. This theory, like many successful conspiracy theories, is built on a grain of truth: Soros did once suggest that wealthy Europe might make a humanitarian gesture and admit more Syrians, in order to help the poorer nations of the Middle East cope with the refugee crisis. But the propaganda in Hungary—and on myriad European and American far-right, white supremacist, and "identitarian" websites—goes far beyond that. It suggests that Soros is the chief instigator of a deliberate Jewish plot to replace white, Christian Europeans—and Hungarians in particular—with brown-skinned Muslims. These movements do not perceive migrants just as an economic burden or even a terrorist threat, but rather as an existential challenge to the nation itself. At various times, the Hungarian government has put Soros's face on posters, on the floors of subway trains, and on leaflets, hoping that it will scare Hungarians into supporting the government.

In Poland, the lie is at least sui generis. It is the Smolensk conspiracy theory, which obsesses our old friend Anita Gargas and so many others: the belief that a nefarious plot brought down the president's plane in

April 2010. The story has special force in Poland because the crash did have eerie historical echoes. The president who died, Lech Kaczyński, was on his way to an event commemorating the Katyń massacres, a series of mass murders that took place in 1940, when Stalin slaughtered more than twenty-one thousand Polish officers—a deliberate assault on what was then the country's elite. Dozens of senior military figures and politicians were also on board, many of them friends of mine. My husband knew almost everybody on the plane, including the flight attendants.

A huge wave of emotion followed the accident. A kind of hysteria, something like the madness that took hold in the United States after 9/11, engulfed the nation. Television announcers wore black mourning ties; friends gathered at our Warsaw apartment to talk about history repeating itself in that dark, damp Russian forest. My own recollection of the days that followed are jumbled and chaotic. I remember going to buy a black suit to wear to the memorial services; I remember one of the widows, so frail she seemed barely able to stand, weeping at her husband's funeral. My own husband, who had refused an invitation to travel with the president on that trip, went out to the airport every evening to stand at attention while the coffins were brought home.

At first the tragedy seemed to unify people; after all, politicians from every major party had been on the plane. The funerals took place all over the country. Even Vladimir Putin, then the Russian prime minister, seemed moved. He went to Smolensk to meet Tusk, then the Polish prime minister, on the evening of the crash. The next day, one of Russia's most-watched television channels broadcast *Katyń,* an emotional and very anti-Soviet Polish film, directed by Andrzej Wajda, Poland's greatest director. Nothing like it has ever been shown so widely in Russia, before or since.

But the crash did not bring people together. Nor did the investigation into its cause.

Teams of Polish experts were on the ground that same day. They did their best to identify bodies. They examined the wreckage. Once the black box was found, they began to transcribe the cockpit tape. The truth, as it began to emerge, was not comforting to Law and Justice or to its leader, the dead president's twin brother. The plane had taken off late; the president was likely in a hurry to land, because he wanted to use the trip to launch his reelection campaign. He may have been up late, and drinking, the night before. As the pilots approached, they learned that there was thick fog in Smolensk, which did not have a real airport, just a landing strip in the forest; they considered diverting the plane, which would have meant a drive of several hours to the ceremony. After the president had a brief phone call with his brother, his advisers apparently pressed the pilots to land. Some of the advisers, against protocol, walked in and out of the cockpit during the flight. Also against protocol, the chief of the air force came and sat beside the pilots. *"Zmieścisz się śmiało"*—"You'll make it, be bold," he said. Seconds later, the plane collided with the tops of some birch trees, rolled over, and hit the ground.

Initially, Jarosław Kaczyński seems to have believed that the crash was an accident. "It's your fault and the fault of the tabloids," he told my husband, who had the horrific task of informing him of the crash. By that, he meant that it was the government's fault because, intimidated by tabloid journalism, it had refused to buy new airplanes. But as the investigation unfolded, its findings were not to his liking. There was nothing wrong with the plane.

Perhaps, like so many people who rely on conspiracy theories to make sense of random tragedies, Kaczyński simply couldn't accept that his beloved brother had died pointlessly; perhaps he could not accept the even more difficult fact that the evidence suggests the president and his team, perhaps even inspired by that phone call, had pressured the pilots to land, thus starting the chain of events that led to the crash. Maybe he felt guilty—the trip was his idea—or remorseful. Or perhaps, like Donald Trump, he saw how a conspiracy theory could help him attain power.

Much as Trump used birtherism to stoke suspicion of the "establishment" even before he was a candidate, Kaczyński used the Smolensk tragedy to galvanize his followers, to reach out to new supporters on the extreme right, to convince them not to trust the government or the media. Sometimes he has implied that the Russian government downed the plane. At other times, he has blamed the former ruling party, now the largest opposition party, for his brother's death: "You destroyed him, you murdered him, you are scum!" he once shouted in parliament.

None of his accusations are true, and at some level he seems to know this. Perhaps to distance himself somewhat from the lies that needed to be told, he gave the job of promoting the conspiracy theory to one of his oldest and strangest comrades. Antoni Macierewicz is a member of Kaczyński's generation, a longtime anti-Communist, though one with some odd Russian connections and strange habits. His secretive demeanor and personal obsessions—he has said that he finds the *Protocols of the Elders of Zion* to be a plausible document—even led the Law and Justice Party to make an election promise in 2015: Macierewicz would definitely not be the defense minister.

But as soon as the party won, Kaczyński broke his promise and appointed Macierewicz to precisely that post. Immediately, Macierewicz began to institutionalize the Smolensk lie. He created a new investigation commission composed of cranks, among them an ethnomusicologist, a retired pilot, a psychologist, a Russian economist, and other people with no expertise on air crashes. The previous official report was removed from a government website. Police entered the homes of the aviation experts who had testified during the original investigation, interrogated them, and confiscated their computers. When Macierewicz went to Washington,

D.C., to meet his American counterparts at the Pentagon, the first thing he did was ask whether U.S. intelligence had any secret information on Smolensk. The reaction was widespread concern about the minister's mental state.

When, some weeks after the election, European institutions and human-rights groups began responding to the actions of the Law and Justice government, they focused on the undermining of the courts and public media. They didn't focus on the institutionalization of the Smolensk conspiracy theory, which was, frankly, just too weird for outsiders to understand. And yet the decision to put a fantasy at the heart of government policy really inspired much of what followed.

Although the Macierewicz commission has never produced a credible alternate explanation for the crash, the Smolensk lie laid the moral groundwork for other lies. Those who could accept this elaborate theory—could accept anything. They could accept the broken promise not to put Macierewicz in the government. They could accept—even though Law and Justice is supposedly a "patriotic" and anti-Russian party—Macierewicz's decisions to fire many of the country's highest military commanders, to cancel weapons contracts, to promote people with Russian links, to raid a NATO facility in Warsaw in the middle of the night. The lie also gave the foot soldiers of the far right an ideological basis for tolerating other offenses. Whatever mistakes the party might make, whatever laws it might break, at least the "truth" about Smolensk would finally be told.

The Smolensk conspiracy theory also served another purpose: for a younger generation that no longer remembered Communism, and for a society where former Communists had largely disappeared from politics, it offered a new reason to distrust the politicians, businesspeople, and intellectuals who had emerged from the struggles of the 1990s and now led the country. More to the point, it offered a means of defining a new and better elite. There was no need for competition, or for exams, or for a résumé bristling with achievements. Anyone who professes belief in the Smolensk lie is by definition a true patriot—and thus qualified for a government job. And Poland is not, of course, the only country where this simple mechanism functions.

The emotional appeal of a conspiracy theory is in its simplicity. It explains away complex phenomena, accounts for chance and accidents, offers the believer the satisfying sense of having special, privileged access to the truth. For those who become the one-party state's gatekeepers, the repetition of these conspiracy theories also brings another reward: power.

Mária Schmidt wasn't at my New Year's Eve party, but I've known her for almost that long. She's a historian, the author of some valuable work on Hungarian

Stalinism; she gave me quite a bit of help when I was writing about Hungarian Stalinism myself. We first met in 2002, when she invited me to the opening of the Terror Háza—the House of Terror museum—in Budapest, which once gave me an award. The museum, which she still directs, explores the history of totalitarianism in Hungary. When it opened, it was one of the most innovative new museums in the eastern half of Europe.

From its first day, the museum has also had harsh critics. Many visitors didn't like the first room, which has a panel of televisions on one wall broadcasting Nazi propaganda, and a panel of televisions on the opposite wall broadcasting Communist propaganda. In 2002, it was still a shock to see the two regimes compared, though perhaps it is less so now. Others felt that the museum gave insufficient weight and space to the crimes of fascism, though Communists ran Hungary for far longer than the fascists did, so there is more to show. I liked the fact that the museum was seeking to reach younger people with its video and audio exhibits, and its intelligent use of objects. I also liked the fact that the museum showed ordinary Hungarians collaborating with both regimes, which I thought might help their descendants understand that their country—like every country—should take responsibility for its own politics and its own history, avoiding the narrow nationalist trap of blaming problems on outsiders.

Yet this is precisely the narrow nationalist trap into which Hungary has now fallen. Hungary's belated reckoning with its Communist past—putting up museums, holding memorial services, naming perpetrators—did not, as I thought it would, help cement respect for the rule of law. On the contrary, sixteen years after the Terror Háza's opening, Hungary's ruling party respects no restraints of any kind. It has gone much further even than Law and Justice in politicizing the state media and destroying the private media, achieving the latter by issuing threats, blocking access to advertising, and then encouraging friendly businessmen to buy up media properties weakened by the harassment and loss of revenue. In addition to a claque of ideologues, the Hungarian government, like the Russian government, has also created a new business elite that is loyal to Orbán, and that benefits accordingly. One Hungarian businessman who preferred not to be named told me that soon after Orbán first took over the government, regime cronies demanded that the businessman sell them his company at a low price; when he refused, they arranged for "tax inspections" and other forms of harassment, as well as a campaign of intimidation that forced him to hire bodyguards. Eventually he, like so many others in the same position, sold his Hungarian property and left the country.

Like the Polish government, the Hungarian state promotes a Medium-Size Lie: it pumps out propaganda blaming Hungary's problems—including the coronavirus, which the country's hospitals were ill-equipped to fight—on nonexistent Muslim migrants, the EU, and, again, George Soros. Despite her opposition credentials and intellectual achievements, Schmidt—a historian, scholar, and museum curator—was one of the primary authors of that lie. She periodically publishes long, angry blog posts fulminating against Soros; against the Central European University, originally founded with his money; and against "left intellectuals," by which she seems to mostly mean liberal democrats, from the center left to the center right.

Ironies and paradoxes in her life story are plentiful. Schmidt herself was a member of the anti-Communist opposition, though not a prominent one. She once told me a story about how, in her university years, all of the opponents of Communism used to work in the same Budapest library; at a certain point, someone would give a signal and all of them would get up and meet for coffee. After 1989, she became a prime beneficiary of Hungary's political transition: her late husband made a fortune in the post-Communist real-estate market, thanks to which she lives in a spectacular house in the Buda hills. Although she has led a publicity campaign designed to undermine the Central European University founded by Soros, her son is one of its graduates. And although she knows very well what happened in her country in the 1940s, she followed, step by step, the Communist Party playbook when she took over *Figyelő,* a once-respected Hungarian magazine: she changed the editors, pushed out the independent reporters, and replaced them with reliably loyal progovernment writers.

Figyelő remained "private property" and thus technically independent. But from the beginning, it wasn't hard to see who was supporting the magazine. An issue that featured an attack on Hungarian NGOs—the cover visually equated them with the Islamic State—also included a dozen pages of government-paid advertisements, for the Hungarian National Bank, the treasury, the official government-funded anti-Soros campaign. This is a modern reinvention of the progovernment, one-party-state press, complete with the same cynical tone that the Communist publications once used. It is a Hungarian version of Jacek Kurski's Polish state television: sneering, crude, vicious. In April 2018 it printed a list of so-called "mercenaries of Soros"—the "traitors" who worked for organizations that had received Soros donations—thus setting them up to be subjects of scorn and attack. In December of that same year, it put András Heisler, the leader of the Hungarian Jewish community, on the cover with banknotes—Hungarian twenty-thousand-forint bills—floating around and over his image.

Schmidt agreed to speak with me—after calling me "arrogant and ignorant"—only if I would listen to her objections to an article, about Hungary and other things, that I had written for *The Washington Post*. Despite this unpromising invitation, I flew to Budapest, where the candid conversation I had hoped for proved impossible. Schmidt speaks excellent English, but she told me that she wanted to use a translator. She produced a terrified-looking young man who, judging by the transcripts, left out chunks of what she said. And though she has known me for nearly two decades, she plunked a tape recorder on the table, in what I assumed was a sign of distrust.

She then proceeded to repeat the same arguments that had appeared in her blog posts. As her main bit of evidence that George Soros "owns" the Democratic Party in the United States, she cited an episode of *Saturday Night Live*. As proof that the United States is "a hard-core ideologically based colonizing power," she cited a speech Barack Obama gave in which he criticized a Hungarian foundation for proposing to build a statue in honor of Bálint Hóman, the man who wrote Hungary's anti-Jewish laws in the 1930s and 1940s. She repeated her claim that immigration poses a dire threat to Hungary and became annoyed when I asked, several times, where all the immigrants were. "They're in Germany," she finally snapped. Of course they are: those few Middle Eastern immigrants who did manage to enter Hungary in 2016 had no desire to stay. Immigration is an imaginary problem in Hungary, not a real one.

Schmidt is touchy, angry: she says she feels patronized, and not only by me. Recently, the writer Ivan Krastev has described this mood, which he has compared to a "post-colonial" mindset. Unimpressed by (or uninterested in) the universal values that underly democracy, some people, especially accomplished intellectuals like Schmidt, now find it humiliating to have been imitators of the Western democratic project rather than founders of something original themselves. In speaking to me, Schmidt used precisely this language. The Western media and Western diplomats "talk down from above to those below like it used to be with colonies," she told me. When Schmidt hears talk of anti-Semitism, corruption, and authoritarianism she instinctively reacts with a version of "it's none of your business."

Yet Schmidt, who spends a lot of time criticizing Western democracy, is not offering anything better or different in its place. Despite being dedicated to the uniqueness of Hungary and the value of "Hungarianness," Schmidt has lifted much of her profoundly unoriginal ideology wholesale from Breitbart News, right down to the caricatured description of American universities and sneering jokes about "transsexual bathrooms." Yet there is no cultural left in Hungary to speak of, and in any case Orbán, who has put the Hungarian Academy of Sciences under direct government control, terrified academics into silence, and forced the Central European University out of the country, is a far greater threat to academic freedom than anyone on the left in his country. I know of at least one group of Hungarian academics who decided not to publish an electoral analysis—it showed that Fidesz had cheated—for fear of losing funding, or losing their jobs. But Mária continues the fight against the nonexistent "left" anyway. She even invited Steve Bannon and Milo Yiannopoulos to Budapest, long after both of those sad figures ceased to have much influence in the United States. Even her alt-right nationalism is, in the end, another imitation.

The other irony is how much she, far more so than Orbán, perfectly embodies the ethos of the Bolsheviks she genuinely hates. Her cynicism is profound. Soros's support for Syrian refugees cannot be philanthropy; it must come from a deep desire to destroy Hungary. Obama's comments about the statue were not sincere; they must have reflected a financial relationship with Soros. Angela Merkel's refugee policy could not possibly have come from a desire to help people; it had another, nefarious agenda. "I think it is just bullshit," Schmidt said. "I would say she wanted to prove that Germans, this time, are the good people. And they can lecture everybody on humanism and morality. It doesn't matter for the Germans what they can lecture the rest of the world on; they just have to lecture someone." All of this recalls Lenin's contempt for the institutions of "bourgeois democracy," for the free press he considered to be phony and the liberal idealism he considered to be inauthentic.

But the Medium-Size Lie is working for Orbán—just as it has for Donald Trump, and for Kaczyński—if only because it focuses the world's attention on his rhetoric rather than his actions. Schmidt and I spent most of our unpleasant two-hour conversation arguing about nonsensical questions: Does George Soros own the Democratic Party? Are the migrants who tried to cross Hungary to get to Germany in 2016—and have now stopped coming altogether—still a threat to the nation, as government

propaganda insists? We spent no time at all discuss-
ing Russia's influence in Hungary, which is now very
strong, or the fact that her museum's special exhibitions
have slowly begun to reflect the new anti-German, anti-
European form of political correctness in the country:
on the anniversary of 1917, for example, she put on an
exhibition that portrayed the Russian revolution as nothing more than a German intelligence operation.

We did not talk about corruption, or the myriad
ways—documented by Reuters, the *Financial Times,* and
others—that Orbán's friends have personally benefited
from European subsidies and legislative sleight of hand.
Orbán's method works: Talk about emotive issues. Set
yourself up as a defender of Western civilization, especially abroad. That way nobody notices the nepotism and
graft at home.

Nor, in the end, did I learn much about Schmidt's
motives. I am sure that her national pride is sincere.
But does she really believe that Hungary is facing a dire
existential threat in the form of George Soros and some
invisible Syrians? Maybe she is one of those people who
can usefully persuade themselves to believe what it is
advantageous to believe. Or maybe she's just as cynical
about her own side as she is about her opponents, and it's
all an elaborate game.

There are advantages to her position. Thanks to
Orbán, Schmidt has had for nearly two decades the
funding and political support needed to oversee not just
her museum but also a pair of historical institutes, giving

her unique power to shape how Hungarians remember their history, a power that she relishes. In this sense she really does recall the French writer Maurice Barrès, one of Julien Benda's *clercs*. Though Barrès "began as an intellectual skeptic," Benda wrote, "his material star waxed a hundredfold greater, at least in his own country, when he made himself the apostle of 'necessary prejudices.'" Barrès adopted extremist, far-right politics—and became rich and famous in the process. Schmidt's angry anticolonialism has helped her too.

Perhaps that's why she plays the game so carefully, always keeping on the right side of the ruling party. After we met, she published on her blog, without my permission, a heavily edited transcript of our conversation, which was confusingly presented as her interview of me and seemed intended to prove that she had "won" our argument. The transcript also appeared on the Hungarian government's official website, in English.

Try to imagine the White House publishing the transcript of a conversation between, say, the head of the Smithsonian Institution and a foreign critic of Trump and you'll understand how strange this is. But when I saw it, I realized why she had agreed to the interview: It had been a performance, designed to prove to other Hungarians that Schmidt is loyal to the regime and willing to defend it. Which she is.

III

The Future of Nostalgia

THE READER WHO has come this far—wading deep into the details of Polish and Hungarian politics, meeting a variety of people with hard-to-pronounce names—may be tempted to dismiss these as merely regional stories. Many may imagine that the crisis of European democracy is some kind of "eastern" problem unique to "former Communist countries" that are still experiencing a hangover from 1989. Some also attribute the new authoritarianism in Eastern Europe to a broader regional failure to grapple with the legacy of the past.

But this explanation is inadequate, for these movements are new. There was no authoritarian-nationalist, antidemocratic wave after 1989 in central Europe, outside of ex-Yugoslavia. It has arisen more recently, in the past decade. And it arose not because of mystical "ghosts from the past" but as the result of specific actions of people who disliked their existing democracies. They disliked them because they were too weak or too imitative, too indecisive or too individualistic—or because they personally were not advancing fast enough within them. There is nothing "eastern" about Jacek Kurski's resentment of his brother's success and his belief that he deserved more. There is nothing "post-Communist" about Mária Schmidt's turn from dissident to sycophant: these are very old stories, and they belong to the West as much as the East. There is nothing special, in this sense, about the lands between Moscow and Berlin.

At a fish restaurant in an ugly square on a beautiful night in Athens, I described my 1999 New Year's Eve party to a Greek political scientist. Quietly, he laughed at me. Or rather, he laughed with me; he didn't mean to be rude. But this thing I was calling polarization was nothing new. "The post-1989 liberal moment—this was the exception," Stathis Kalyvas said. Unity is an anomaly. Polarization is normal. Skepticism about liberal democracy is also normal. And the appeal of authoritarianism is eternal.

Kalyvas is, among other things, the author of several well-known books about civil wars, including Greece's 1940s civil war, one of many moments in European history when radically divergent political groups took up arms and started to kill one another. But *civil war* and *civil peace* are relative terms in Greece at the best of times. A vicious military junta ruled the country between 1967 and 1974; there were violent riots in Athens in 2008; a few years later, a far-left party was in power, in coalition with a far-right party. As we were speaking, Greece was having a centrist moment. It was suddenly fashionable to be "liberal," lots of people in Athens told me, by which they meant neither Communist nor authoritarian. Cutting-edge young people were calling themselves "neo-liberal," adopting a term that had been anathema only a few years earlier. This fashion turned out to matter: a year after my visit, a centrist liberal, Kyriakos Mitsotakis, actually won the Greek elections and became prime minister.

Still, even the most optimistic centrists were not convinced that this change would last. "We survived the left-wing extremists," several people reflected gloomily, "and now we are bracing for the right-wing extremists." A nasty argument had long been brewing about the status of Northern Macedonia, the former Yugoslav republic neighboring Greece; soon after I left, the Greek government expelled some Russian diplomats for trying to foment anti-Macedonia hysteria in the northern part of the country. Whatever equilibrium your nation reaches, there is always someone, at home or abroad, who has reasons to upset it.

In Greece, history feels circular. Now there is liberal democracy. But next, there might be oligarchy; then there could be liberal democracy again. Then there may be foreign subversion, an attempted coup, a civil war, a dictatorship, or maybe oligarchy again. That's how it will be because that's how it's always been, all the way back to the original Athenian republic.

History suddenly feels circular in other parts of Europe

too. The divide that has shattered Poland resembles the divide that split Weimar Germany. The language used by the European radical right—the demand for "revolution" against "elites," the dreams of "cleansing" violence and an apocalyptic cultural clash—is eerily similar to the language once used by the European radical left. The presence of dissatisfied, discontented intellectuals—people who feel that the rules aren't fair and that the wrong people have influence—isn't even uniquely European. Moisés Naím, the Venezuelan writer, visited Warsaw a few months after the Law and Justice Party came to power. He asked me to describe the new Polish leaders: What were they like, as people? I gave him some adjectives—*angry, vengeful, resentful.* "They sound just like Chavistas," he told me. I visited Venezuela at the beginning of 2020 and was struck by the myriad ways in which it resembled not just the old Marxist-Leninist states, but also the new nationalist regimes. Economic catastrophe and a hushed-up, covered-up famine on the one hand; attacks on the rule of law, on the press, on academia, and on mythical "elites" on the other. State television broadcast repetitive propaganda and blatant lies; polarization was so deep that it was visible in the very geography of Caracas. In that sense, the city reminded me not only of Eastern Europe in the past, but of some parts of the Western world in the present.

When people have rejected aristocracy, no longer believe that leadership is inherited at birth, no longer assume that the ruling class is endorsed by God, the argument about who gets to rule—who is the elite—is never over. For a long time, some people in Europe and North America settled on the idea that various forms of democratic, meritocratic, and economic competition are the fairest alternative to inherited or ordained power. But even in countries that were never occupied by the Red Army and never ruled by Latin American populists, democracy and free markets can produce unsatisfying outcomes, especially when badly regulated, or when nobody trusts the regulators, or when people are entering the contest from very different starting points. The losers of these competitions were always, sooner or later, going to challenge the value of the competition itself.

More to the point, the principles of competition, even when they encourage talent and create upward mobility, don't answer deeper questions about national or personal identity. They don't satisfy the desire for unity and harmony. Above all, they do not satisfy the desire of some to belong to a special community, a unique community, a *superior* community. This is not just a problem for Poland, or Hungary, or Venezuela, or Greece. It can happen in some of the oldest and most secure democracies in the world.

I first met Boris Johnson on a long-ago evening in Brussels, in the company of my husband, a friend of Johnson's from Oxford—although *friend* is an ambiguous term here. To be more precise, they were both members of the

Bullingdon Club, a unique Oxford institution that flourished in the *Brideshead Revisited* revival era of the 1980s, when Merchant and Ivory were making *Heat and Dust,* and Princess Diana was married at St. Paul's Cathedral. I am not sure that members of the Bullingdon were necessarily "friends": they were rivals, they were drinking partners, but I don't think many of them cry on one another's shoulders when times are tough.

Had it not produced two prime ministers—Johnson and David Cameron—as well as a chancellor of the exchequer, the Bullingdon would have faded away into deserved obscurity after the Merchant Ivory era ended and the Prince and Princess of Wales got divorced. Even in the 1980s it was already shading into parody, having been mocked half a century earlier in Evelyn Waugh's 1928 novel *Decline and Fall.* That book begins with a famous description of the annual meeting of the "Bollinger Club":

> A shriller note could now be heard rising from Sir Alistair's rooms; any who have heard that sound will shrink at the recollection of it; it is the sound of the English county families, baying for broken glass. . . .

I know for a fact that some of Johnson's fellow members are now deeply embarrassed by the Bullingdon, with its Regency dandy's uniform—tailcoat, yellow silk waistcoat, blue bow tie—its drunken, champagne-fueled meetings, its reputation for breaking furniture as well as windows, and its pretentious links, or rather pretended links, to the old aristocracy. But others, and I think both my husband and Johnson fall into this category, remembered it as a kind of extended joke. With a few exceptions, most of the members were not actually aristocrats, or if they were, then not terribly grand ones. Johnson himself is the son of an EU bureaucrat and grew up partly in Brussels. Radek was a refugee from Communist Poland, albeit one gifted with a British sense of humor. Both were playing with the old forms of the English class system, acting out some of the roles because it amused them. They enjoyed the Bullingdon not despite Waugh's vicious parody, but because of it.

When we had that dinner with Johnson, he was in Brussels as the correspondent for the *Daily Telegraph,* the house newspaper of the British Tory party. After a couple of years in the job he had already made a name for himself. His specialty was amusing, half-true stories built around a grain (or sometimes less than a grain) of fact that poked fun at the EU and invariably portrayed it as a font of regulatory madness. His articles had titles like "Threat to British Pink Sausages." They repeated (false) rumors that Brussels bureaucrats were going to ban double-decker buses or prawn-cocktail-flavored crisps. Although they were laughed at by those in the know, these tall tales had an impact. Other editors demanded that their Brussels correspondents find and file the same kinds of stories; the tabloids raced to keep up. Year after year, these kinds of stories helped to build the distrust for the EU that paved the way, many years later, for Brexit. Johnson was well aware of the impact and relished it. "I was sort of chucking these rocks over the garden wall and I listened to this amazing crash from the greenhouse next door over in England," he told the BBC years later, in an extraordinarily candid interview: "everything I wrote from Brussels was having this amazing, explosive effect on the Tory party—and it really gave me this, I suppose, rather weird sense of power."

The "amazing crash" in London also sold newspapers, which is part of why Johnson was laughingly tolerated for so long. But there was a deeper reason too: the not-entirely-accurate stories appealed to the deep instincts of a certain breed of nostalgic conservative, readers and editors of the *Daily Telegraph,* the *Sunday Telegraph,* and their sister publication, the *Spectator* magazine, all three of which were then owned by the same Canadian busi-nessman, Conrad Black. I knew this world very well. At different times, I wrote a column for the *Telegraph* and the *Sunday Telegraph;* I worked at the *Spectator,* eventually as deputy editor, from 1992 until 1996, in an era when the magazine was run by Dominic Lawson, a brilliant editor, still one of the best I've ever had. At that time, the *Spec-tator* had shabby offices in Doughty Street, unrenovated for decades. But our summer parties and afternoon-long lunches nevertheless attracted an eccentric range of grand guests, from Alec Guinness and Clive James to Auberon Waugh—Evelyn's son—and the Duchess of Devonshire.

In that era, the tone of every conversation, every editorial meeting, was arch, every professional conversation amusing; there was no moment when the joke ended or the irony ceased. Even the straightest articles had fabulously witty headlines. Lawson came up with the one I remember best, for what was no doubt meant to be a deadly serious article about Poland: "Gdansking on Thin Ice." This was an unusual historical moment, one in which Enoch Powell, a controversial anti-immigration Tory politician of a previous generation, was simultaneously an occasional lunch guest, a revered authority—and also, somehow, a figure of fun. There were Tory journalists and Tory MPs who would compete with one another around the dinner table over who could do the best "Enoch" imitations. Maybe they still do.

It would be profoundly inaccurate to say that the circle of people who gravitated around the *Spectator*—if they could be said to be doing something so enthusiastic as to "gravitate"—was actually nostalgic for Britain's imperial past. Nobody, in the 1990s, wished to have India back, and nobody does now. But there was a nostalgia for something else: a world in which England made the rules. Or maybe the expression "nostalgia" is incorrect, because my friends in and around the *Spectator* did not think that they were looking backward. They believed that it was still possible for England to make the rules—whether the rules of trade, of economics, of foreign policy—if only their leaders would take the bull by the horns, take the bit between their teeth, if only they would just do it.

At base, I now think that this was what they really liked about Margaret Thatcher: the fact that she would go out into the world and make things happen. They liked it when she swung her handbag at the Europeans, demanded a rebate from the EU budget, sent a task force to retake the Falkland Islands. Some of what she achieved turned out to be either purely symbolic or not particularly useful—the Falklands being a piece of territory no one has visited or thought much about since the war ended—but it was that act of defiance, that determination to be the decider and not just the negotiator, that really won their admiration.

At the time, I thought that my friends also believed in spreading democracy and free trade across Europe, and perhaps they did. Certainly Thatcher did. The fight against Communism was a real battle that, both rhetorically and geostrategically, she helped to win. The European Single Market—the vast European trading zone where regulations are coordinated so that the manufacture and exchange of goods is seamless across the continent—was actually a Thatcherite idea, and very much the product of UK diplomacy. It remains the deepest and most profound free-trade agreement ever conceived, which is precisely why the protectionist left wing of the European political spectrum always hated it.

More recently I have come to suspect that "democracy," at least as an international cause, was far less important to a certain kind of nostalgic conservative than the maintenance of a world in which England continued to play a privileged role: a world in which England is not just an ordinary, middle-sized power like France or Germany; a world in which England is *special*—and perhaps even superior. That was part of why some of the nostalgic conservatives were always suspicious of the Single Market that Britain did so much to create. The idea that England, the only European country that, they believed, has a real claim to victory in the Second World War—the country that was never invaded, never surrendered, the country that chose the right side from the beginning—could, in the twenty-first century, make its regulations only in conjunction with other European countries, was simply unacceptable. And I do mean England, not Britain. Although in the 1990s the British were still fighting the IRA in Belfast and my Tory friends were still calling themselves "Unionists," English nationalism was already growing alongside the Scottish nationalism that would eventually lead to Scottish devolution and calls for Scottish independence a few years later.

In retrospect, it is clear that much of what my friends said and wrote at that time about the Single Market was, like Johnson's *Telegraph* columns, fanciful. Nobody in the EU imposed rules on Britain: European directives are agreed by negotiation and each one of them has been accepted by a British representative or diplomat. Although the United Kingdom did not win every single argument—no country did—there was no "Brussels mafia" forcing Britain to do things it didn't want to do.

Though this was rarely mentioned, the Single Market had many advantages, even when the British sometimes lost arguments. It made Britain one of the most powerful players in the world's most powerful economic bloc, it gave Britain an outsized voice in matters of international trade, and it was particularly good for British entrepreneurs. Its success eventually proved to be a magnet for the new democracies of the East, helping to draw the former Communist world into an integrated Europe too. But none of those advantages outweighed, in the end, the embarrassment and annoyance of having to negotiate regulations with other Europeans, a give-and-take process that did, of course, sometimes force the British to make concessions.

Paradoxically, this same group of people were extremely happy to work in partnership, even as a very junior partner, with the United States. In part it was because the United States speaks English and has its historical roots in Great Britain. In part, this was also because the United States, unlike Germany or France, was a real superpower, and some of that reflected glory beamed back at the United Kingdom and flattered its leaders. "We are Greeks to their Romans," said an earlier Tory prime minister, Harold Macmillan, rather smugly, back in the 1960s. Even today, the British spend a lot of time thinking and writing about the so-called "special relationship" between the United States and the United Kingdom—*special relationship* being a phrase much used in London and barely mentioned in Washington, D.C.

Tory grandees could be dismissive of American politics, and downright snobby about American pop culture. They were also quietly skeptical of American foreign policy. Graham Greene's novel *The Quiet American,* with its portrait, simultaneously fond and cruel, of an overenthusiastic American idealist in Vietnam, is perhaps the best expression of this complicated ambivalence. Nevertheless, America was a large partner, a global partner, a fitting partner for the exceptional English. If the Americans were keen on spreading democracy, then the English were happy to join them.

When I arrived in London in the early 1990s, I was granted honorary membership in the world of the nostalgic conservatives partly, perhaps, because I represented the American alliance that was then in vogue. I had lived for a few years in Poland, had written about the fall of Communism and the politics of the post-Communist world. I was also a useful foil, an earnest foreigner, the person always trying to get my English colleagues to stop making jokes and write about difficult foreign places like Russia or China ("We need something serious in this issue: let's get Anne to write it"). Mostly I stayed away from the UK-EU arguments, because others were so much more passionate about them. Once, I did go to Brussels to write about the Conservative Party's members of the European Parliament and discovered that most of them were excellent legislators, knowledgeable and conscientious. But the more successful they were—the more effective they were at reforming and improving Europe, and in making its democratic institutions work—the more their party hated them. "Torture a Tory," I concluded: "Make him an MEP." Even back then, the Conservatives were beginning to divide into those who wanted the EU to be more successful and more representative, and those who just wanted out.

Johnson—born in the United States like me, and very attuned to American ideas—also flourished in that somewhat sleepy, eccentric world. Indeed, he was one of its real stars, capable of finding something amusing to say about a dull European summit one day and of entertaining an audience on a TV quiz program the next. But at some point, both of us began to look for other things to do. I moved back to Poland in 1997 and started writing history books; he ran for Parliament. Later, he became mayor of London, but he got bored there too. In 2013 he told an interviewer that the mayor's office felt far away from the House of Commons, the place where real things happened: "I'm so isolated, I'm like Colonel Kurtz. I've gone upriver," he said, before hastily assuring the interviewer that that was the only thing he had in common with the psychopathic hero of *Apocalypse Now*. In the same interview he repeated a rugby metaphor that he had used before. As always, Johnson said that he wasn't actively trying to take over his party's leadership—but "if the ball came loose in the scrum" he wouldn't mind picking it up.

Quite a lot of people have since remarked on Johnson's outsized narcissism, which is indeed all-consuming, as well as his equally remarkable laziness. His penchant for fabrication is a matter of record. He was fired from the *Times* (London) at the beginning of his career for making up quotes, and fired from the shadow cabinet in 2004 for lying. His aura of carefully studied helplessness also hides a streak of cruelty: Johnson wrecked first one and then another marriage—the second one had lasted a quarter century—and the lives of a number of other women with a series of extraordinarily brazen public affairs.

But there is no point denying that he also has an uncanny form of charisma, some genius quality that attracts people and puts them at ease, as well as an intuitive grasp of the mood of a crowd. Once, after not seeing him for several years, I ran into him somewhere in the City, London's financial district. He was then mayor; he was riding his bike. I waved at him, he stopped, exclaimed over the amazing coincidence, and suggested that we go into a pub for a quick drink. As we opened the door, he mumbled something like "Oh no, I forgot this would happen" as people swarmed over toward us and began demanding selfies. He did a few; then we sat down and chatted; then, when he got up, the same thing happened all over again.

Two other encounters with Johnson stick in my head, also from when he was mayor. In 2014, I heard him give a speech about ancient Athens. Unlike many of his ad hoc public pronouncements, this lecture had real coherence, perhaps because he'd written it down in advance.

Waving a glass of red wine in his hand, he praised Athens in some detail, speaking of its "culture of freedom, openness, and tolerance, intellectual experimentation and democracy," making a clear analogy to modern London. In contrast, he also spoke of Sparta, pointing out that, as Pericles predicted, that harsh, conformist, militaristic society left no elegant ruins in its wake. He warned against the new Spartans and spoke of "the challenge, global in its extent, to democratic freedoms" posed by new authoritarians. People applauded, genuinely moved.

Round about the same time, I went out to dinner with Johnson and a couple of other people, and we wound up talking about a possible referendum on British membership in the EU, which was then in the air. "Nobody serious wants to leave the EU," he said. "Business doesn't want it. The City [London's financial district] doesn't want it. It won't happen." This was how he spoke when he was the liberal mayor of a great, modern, multicultural British city, one that flourished thanks to its deep connections to the outside world.

Nevertheless, he chose Brexit in the referendum campaign. And he supported Brexit with the same sunny insouciance, and the same disregard for consequences, that he had long demonstrated in his journalism and his personal life. He went on telling jokes and stories. He calculated that Brexit would lose. He texted David Cameron, the prime minister: "Brexit will be crushed like a toad under the harrow." But supporting it would, he thought, make him a hero among the Eurosceptic

Tories whom his writing had done so much to cultivate. And in a sense, his calculation came out right, though perhaps not in the way he expected.

In the "normal" progress of events—in a world without Brexit—Boris Johnson might never have become prime minister. The party that elected David Cameron—a moderate centrist, dedicated to "detoxifying" the Tory party after a series of angry-sounding leaders—would have had trouble choosing someone as risky as Johnson, with his history of gaffes, sackings, and sex scandals. Johnson became party leader because the party didn't know what else to do. The rugby scrum had taken place, and someone had indeed dropped the ball.

The desperation began after the referendum in 2016, whose result did not surprise me. A few nights before the vote I was at a dinner party where everyone wrote down their predictions, with a case of wine promised to the winner. I guessed that "Leave"—as in "Leave the EU"—would win by 52–48. It did. I never had the heart to pick up the wine because the dinner party host had worked hard on the "Remain" campaign and was devastated by the result. But the Tory party was definitely surprised. The Tory leadership—the Lords, the party bosses, the parliamentary whips, the Central Office, those who wanted Brexit and those who didn't—was totally unprepared even to think about leaving the EU, the organization that had formed and shaped the British economy, British diplomacy, and Britain's role in the world since the 1970s. So was Johnson.

By 2019, the situation was much worse: The Tories had endured three years of catastrophic leadership under Theresa May, another person who would, in the ordinary course of things, probably never have become prime minister. Very quickly, she fulfilled everybody's worst expectations, making a whole series of unforgivable mistakes. She triggered Article 50, the legal mechanism for leaving the EU—a decision that set a two-year clock ticking—before understanding what Brexit really entailed. She called an unnecessary parliamentary election in 2017 and lost her majority. Worst of all, she set the terms for the destructive Brexit debate. At the very beginning, May could have observed that the referendum had been very close, that Britain's commercial and political ties to Europe were very strong, and that it would make sense for the United Kingdom to carry out an "intelligent" Brexit, and not a "foolish" one: the UK could stay within the Single Market, a British idea, or at the very least within a customs union.

Instead, using the polarizing language of "hard" and "soft" Brexit, she opted for the former and chose to leave both of those institutions. Her decision was instantly applauded by all those who wanted Britain to shout louder in the world. It also triggered, just at the moment when many English Tories had lost interest in Belfast, the unresolvable problem of the border between Northern Ireland and the Republic of Ireland. Because both the north and the south of the island of Ireland had been in the EU, there wasn't actually a border anymore. The

Irish government, with EU backing, refused to allow one now to be built—but this meant that either all of the United Kingdom had to stay within some form of customs union with the EU, or else Northern Ireland would have to follow different rules from the rest of the United Kingdom.

Each one of those solutions was unacceptable to somebody. The wrangling went on for months and months. After consulting with nobody and making no effort to reach across the aisle to other political parties, after displaying a lack of anything resembling political skill, May failed to get her withdrawal deal approved by Parliament in three separate votes, postponed Brexit twice, and then resigned.

The Tories began shedding support and were nearly wiped out in European parliamentary elections in May 2019. Only four forlorn, still-tortured Tory MEPs remained. The party needed a new leader, one who could bring the various wings of the party together, deliver Brexit, win back support. They also needed someone who could tell stories, make them laugh, bring back that feeling of English superiority. They went for the joker.

Nostalgics, the Russian artist and essayist Svetlana Boym wrote in her elegant book *The Future of Nostalgia,* come in two forms. Some are captivated by what she called the "reflective" nostalgia of the émigré or the aesthete, the nostalgia that appeals to collectors of yellowed letters and sepia photographs, the nostalgia of those who like old churches even if they never go to services. Reflective nostalgics miss the past and dream about the past. Some of them study the past and even mourn the past, especially their own personal past. But they do not really want the past back. Perhaps this is because, deep down, they know that the old homestead is in ruins, or because it has been gentrified beyond recognition—or because they quietly recognize that they wouldn't much like it now anyway. Once upon a time life might have been sweeter or simpler, but it was also more dangerous, or more boring, or perhaps more unjust.

Radically different from the reflective nostalgics are what Boym calls the restorative nostalgics, not all of whom recognize themselves as nostalgics at all. Restorative nostalgics don't just look at old photographs and piece together family stories. They are mythmakers and architects, builders of monuments and founders of nationalist political projects. They do not merely want to contemplate or learn from the past. They want, as Boym puts it, to "rebuild the lost home and patch up the memory gaps." Many of them don't recognize their own fictions about the past for what they are: "They believe their project is about truth." They are not interested in a nuanced past, in a world in which great leaders were flawed men, in which famous military victories had lethal side effects. They don't acknowledge that the past might have had its drawbacks. They want the cartoon version of history, and more importantly, they want to live in it, right now. They don't want to act out roles from the past because it amuses them: they want to behave as they think their ancestors did, without irony.

It is not by accident that restorative nostalgia often goes hand in hand with conspiracy theories and the medium-sized lies. These needn't be as harsh or crazy as the Smolensk conspiracy theory or the Soros conspiracy theory; they can gently invoke scapegoats rather than a full-fledged alternative reality. At a minimum, they can offer an explanation: The nation is no longer great because someone has attacked us, undermined us, sapped our strength. Someone—the immigrants, the foreigners, the elites, or indeed the EU—has perverted the course of history and reduced the nation to a shadow of its former self. The essential identity that we once had has been taken away and replaced with something cheap and artificial. Eventually, those who seek power on the back of restorative nostalgia will begin to cultivate these conspiracy theories, or alternative histories, or alternative fibs, whether or not they have any basis in fact.

The concept of "restorative nostalgia" is related to other emotions. German American historian Fritz Stern (himself a "migrant": his Jewish family left Breslau for New York in 1937) also wrote about a parallel phenomenon, which he called something else: "cultural despair." In his very first book, published in the 1960s, he wrote short biographies of several men, all nineteenth-century Germany intellectuals—all living in a period of intense social, political, and economic change—who were afflicted by it. One of them was an obscure German art historian, Julius Langbehn, whose own book *Rembrandt as Educator* began like this:

> It has gradually become an open secret that the contemporary spiritual life of the German people is in a state of slow decay; according to some, even of rapid decay. Science everywhere has dissipated into specialization; in the field of thought and literature, epoch-making individuals are missing. . . . Without question the democratizing, leveling, atomistic tendency of this country expresses itself in all this. . . .

Published in 1890, Langbehn's portrait of the Dutch painter wasn't biography or a critique; it was, rather, a quasi-philosophical tract, an extended polemic. Rembrandt, in Langbehn's vision, represented an ideal, "the highest form of life, art and individuality." He also represented something that was lost: By contrast to Rembrandt, modern men, especially modern Germans, were "pygmies," men with no connection to the past or to the soil. They were "democrats" in a pejorative sense, run-of-the-mill men with no ideals, no dreams, no talent.

Nor did Langbehn have much faith in the leading minds of his age. He disliked science, technology, and modernity. He preferred art, spontaneity, and a more authentic existence of the kind he believed Rembrandt had lived. He disliked Jews, especially secular Jews, who he wrote had "no religion, no character, no home," because they symbolized the rootlessness of contemporary life. But this was not his most important theme. His book was permeated with nostalgia for a different, better time, a time when men were active and not passive, a time when great leaders could make their mark on the world. Though chaotically written, and only distantly related to the actual life of the artist, *Rembrandt as Educator* was a runaway bestseller. It struck a chord in rapidly industrializing late-nineteenth-century Germany, contributing to a wave of restorative nostalgia long before the mass violence of the First World War and the humiliating defeat that followed.

At some point between the 1990s and the 2010s, a number of thoughtful British Tories—journalists, writers, some politicians—were also gripped by something strongly resembling the cultural despair that Stern identified in Langbehn. This began to happen well before the Brexit referendum. I date it to the end of Thatcherism, which coincided with the end of the Cold War, a more momentous turning point for Britain, in retrospect, than we understood at the time. The conflict with Communism had offered British conservatives, in concert with their American allies, the chance to take part in a very successful moral crusade; in 1989, when the Berlin Wall fell and Communist regimes rapidly crumbled, they felt vindicated. Cold Warriors had been unpopular. They had been jeered by the left, including many of their peers at universities, in the press, and in politics. But they had kept the faith. Now they had proof that Thatcher was right. Together they had fought against those who had been fascinated by Communism—and they had won.

But once it was over there was a vacuum. All other causes suddenly seemed less important, less glamorous. Prime Minister John Major, who followed Thatcher, held office for seven years and, like President George H. W. Bush, played an important role in reuniting postwar Europe. But although Major was a self-made man of the kind they said they admired, as well as someone who also spoke evocatively, even nostalgically, of the English past, the nostalgic conservatives hated him. Some of that might have been snobbery: Major never went to university. But they also hated him because, unlike Thatcher, he didn't try to lead a moral crusade. He didn't tout a transformative economic reform program or call for revolutionary change. After the turbulence of the Thatcher years, he thought that governing quietly, from right of center, in cooperation with European allies as well as the United States, was enough. He was sufficiently popular in the country to be reelected in 1992, but he inspired no great admiration among what should have been his intellectual base. At Conrad Black's election night party at the Savoy hotel I watched an unenthusiastic crowd of Conservative editors and Tory party donors eating oysters, sipping champagne, and murmuring their surprise.

The election of Tony Blair cast the reflective nostalgics in the Conservative Party even further into the shadows.

Blair was, in many ways, Thatcher's most important pupil, as Thatcher's biographer, Charles Moore, has made clear. He accepted the need for free markets, he adopted her partnership with the United States, he took the Labour Party to the center and kept it in power for twelve years. But he didn't have an ounce of any kind of nostalgia in his body. He didn't care about the specialness of England. Instead, Blair touted his modernity, embraced social change, encouraged Britain's economic integration with Europe and the world, and devolved power away from London by creating a Scottish parliament and a Welsh assembly, weakening England's voice in national politics. He agreed to a series of compromises that ended the long-standing conflict in Northern Ireland. Among other things, he succeeded because people in the north who felt themselves to be "Irish" can have Irish passports. This blurring of sovereignty finally brought peace.

For the nostalgic conservatives, Blair was a disaster. The triumphant mood of the 1980s gave way to real anger. Almost nobody was angrier than Simon Heffer, a brilliant historian and columnist, the deputy editor of the *Spectator* in the early 1990s—my direct predecessor in that job—and, for a long time, a generous and loyal friend. Simon, whose love for English literature, English film, and English music is deep and genuine, took me to the only county cricket match I've ever attended and introduced me to the Ealing Comedies, a set of droll, literate English movies made in the 1940s and 1950s, some of which I watched at his house. I am the godmother of one of his children, just as Ania Bielecka is the godmother to one of mine. Much of the time we worked together he was energetically, though still relatively cheerfully, attacking John Major, the EU, and the state of modern Britain. By the mid-2000s, when I was out of Britain and saw him only occasionally, several years of Labour Party leadership had made him apoplectic with rage. In 2006—a moment when it was hard to imagine how any Conservative leader would ever be able to defeat the Labour Party, ever again—he wrote, for example, that, "thanks to a happy accident of birth, I was only nine and a half when the 1960s finished":

> I say happy, because when I survey a country run by people 10 years older than me, and who are still fixated by the dope-smoking, peace-and-love, hairy hippy self-indulgence for which that dismal decade is famed, I thank God I escaped. . . . Our Government of former student political activists . . . remains utterly hamstrung by its own teenage prejudices, and utterly boring about them. And the damage these people, in their lack of wisdom, inflict on society is still enormous, and every bit as corrosive as the scourge of drugs about which, until now, they have been so casual.

Nor was the problem just drugs. All around him he saw decline: rising political correctness, as well as a "savage crime wave." Most of all, Heffer wrote, in the spirit of Langbehn, "the idea of merit has gone out of public life." Just like his German predecessor, he mourned the fact that the modern age no longer produced great leaders. There were no Churchills, no Thatchers, just the "dope-smoking, peace-and-love, hairy hippy self-indulgence" of Tony Blair's Labour Party. Even when the Conservatives finally returned to office, his faith in modern leadership was not renewed. Soon after David Cameron's selection as Tory party leader, Heffer wrote that Cameron had "never exhibited the slightest scintilla of principle at any time during his political career." He then repeated some version of that same sentence in many articles for the next seven years, right up to the moment of the Brexit referendum campaign. He supported Leave and called Cameron a "liar," a month before the vote. In the same article, he denounced the United Kingdom as a "banana republic" with worthless institutions.

Heffer might have been uniquely vitriolic, but his underlying frustration was not unique at all. In that same era, Roger Scruton, a great conservative philosopher and another old friend, wrote a book called *England: An Elegy*, which was genuinely touching, beautifully written, and even more profoundly apocalyptic than Heffer's journalism. I met Scruton in the late 1980s, when he ran a charity that sent money to dissidents in Eastern Europe using students, and others, as couriers; I became one of them. I knew him as a brave critic of Communism at a time when that was not a fashionable thing to be. But *England: An Elegy* has a different theme. Scruton began by explaining that the book would "pay a personal tribute to the civilization that made me and which is now passing from the world." This was not an analysis or a history: it was "a funeral oration," an "attempt to understand, from a philosophical perspective, what we are losing as our form of life decays." The elegantly composed chapters that followed paid tribute to what was, he said, a dead or dying England: English culture, English religion, English laws, and English character. This was classic, reflective nostalgia, and it finished with an extraordinary outpouring of cultural despair:

> The old England for which our parents fought has been reduced to isolated pockets between the motorways. The family farm, which maintained the small-scale and diversified production that was largely responsible for the shape and appearance of England, is now on the verge of extinction. The towns have lost their centres, which are boarded up and vandalized; and the cities have been all but obliterated by vast steel structures which at night stand empty amid the wastes of illuminated concrete. The night sky is no longer visible, but everywhere blanketed with a sickly orange glow, and England is becoming a no-man's land, an "elsewhere," managed by executives who visit the

outposts only fleetingly, staying in multinational hotels on the edges of floodlit wastelands.

Scruton's love of the countryside, his lifelong advocacy of premodern architectural styles, and his faith in communities and local institutions could have led him to support the EU, whose policies explicitly seek to protect and promote European products and trademarks, to preserve European architecture and agriculture—and with it, the European countryside—sometimes in the teeth of market forces. He might have called for the EU to do more of these things, or to do them better; he might have come to see the EU, as so many Europeans do, as a bulwark against a world increasingly dominated by China, the United States, and global companies and banks with no interest in small European towns like the ones Scruton loved. But he, like Heffer and many others, came to the opposite conclusion.

In due course, the EU became a kind of fixation for the nostalgic conservatives. Quite apart from any legitimate criticisms of EU policies or behaviors—and of course there are many to be made—"Europe" became, for some of them, the embodiment of everything else that had gone wrong, the explanation for the toothlessness of the ruling class, the mediocrity of British culture, the ugliness of modern capitalism, and the general lack of national vigor. The need to negotiate regulations had emasculated the British Parliament. The Polish plumbers and Spanish data analysts working in Britain were not fellow Europeans who shared a common culture but immigrants threatening the nation's identity. As time passed, these views became ever more deeply felt—so much so that they slowly created new cleavages, altered relationships, changed minds. In 2012, my husband made a speech at a conference begging Britain not just to stay in the EU but to lead it. The EU, he said, "is an English-speaking power. The Single Market was a British idea. . . . You could, if you only wished, lead Europe's defence policy." The speech was reprinted in the *Times;* Heffer wrote me an angry note about it. I later wrote him some angry notes too, and for a long time we didn't speak to each other.

To those in England—and they were mostly in England, not Scotland, Wales or Northern Ireland—who saw the world through this prism, the fight against "Europe" slowly took on the character of a valiant conflict, with clear echoes from the past. Popular culture had already established the Second World War as the central event in modern history, and the Brexit campaign fit beautifully into this story. Two films about Churchill and one about Dunkirk were released in the lull between the referendum and Brexit. Andrew Roberts's Churchill biography became a bestseller in 2018; Johnson's own biography of Churchill had done very well a few years before. William Cash, a Tory MP who dedicated his career to pulling Britain out of Europe, compared Britain's EU membership to "appeasement" in a 2016 interview. In the same interview, he alluded to the memory of his father, who died on the Normandy beaches, while explaining why he didn't want to live in a "German-run Europe" today. In the final column that he wrote before the referendum, Heffer described the EU, an organization that Britain had helped lead for two generations, as "a foreign power overruling [our] courts and [our] elected government." He described the Leave campaigners as representatives of an "upsurge of national consciousness that we have not known since the Second World War." Invoking the spirit of the Blitz, he declared: "This is our moment of greatness."

This turn toward restorative nostalgia led Heffer to reject the Conservative Party long before 2016. At some point in the 1990s, he told me he would cast a vote for the UK Independence Party, the one-issue political movement that sought to extract Britain from the EU, though of course I don't know if he actually did; I remember being surprised because at that time I had never heard of UKIP, which was then a very fringe organization. UKIP functioned, in practice, as the party of English nationalism, its real interest being as much English resurgence as British "independence." UKIP's founder and leader, Nigel Farage, was a wealthy City trader, a stockbroker's son who wore tweed jackets, had himself photographed drinking beer in pubs, and, hypocritically, claimed to speak for the common man and against the "elite." He did not share Scruton's Burkean, elegiac nostalgia; he took Heffer's anger at the people who ran Britain and put it to political use. He was not an intellectual by any means, but he was someone who, like one of Benda's *clercs,* molded and shaped other people's ideas into a political project. The Tories at first condemned him. Then, as UKIP's star rose, they sought to copy him.

Sometimes there was a racial undertone to this kind of English nationalism: by definition, there can be no black "Englishmen," even if there can be black Britons. But this was really not about the color of anyone's skin. The concept of "Englishness" also excluded the British Irish of Belfast, after all, as well as the British Scots of Glasgow and everyone else in the United Kingdom's Gaelic fringe. Its adherents even came to believe that if leaving the EU broke up the United Kingdom—and they always knew it might—then so be it. John O'Sullivan, a former speechwriter for Margaret Thatcher, was willing to pay that price too. "Oh, Scotland will go," O'Sullivan told me years ago, "and we will carry on."

For some, the potential for constitutional and political chaos was not just a regrettable side effect: it was part of the Brexit appeal. Dressed in hoodies and dark sunglasses, Dominic Cummings affected a completely different style from the tweed-encased nostalgic conservatives, with their brogues and Barbour jackets. As far as I know, he has never expressed any longing for the past at all. But sociologically, Cummings—one of the chief spin doctors of the Leave campaign, and then Johnson's primary adviser—was closely related to the nostalgic conservatives. He was the husband of a *Spectator* editor, the son-in-law of a baronet, the nephew of a famous judge with an Oxford humanities degree. More importantly, he shared a part of their sensibility, especially their belief that something essential about England was dead and gone. In the run-up to the Brexit campaign and in the months afterward, Cummings wrote a series of blog posts, bristling with tech-speak and military jargon, that poured scorn on the British Parliament, British politicians, and the British civil service using very different language from Heffer but deploying exactly the same level of fury. He wrote of the "systemic dysfunction of our institutions and the influence of grotesque incompetents," and described British policy-making as "the blind leading the blind."

Although he would never have called himself one, Cummings saw Europe in the same terms as the other restorative nostalgics. In one of his online essays, posted in 2019, before Boris Johnson made him chief special adviser, Cummings excoriated the EU for holding Britain back: "The old institutions like the UN and EU—built on early twentieth century assumptions about the performance of centralised bureaucracies—are incapable of solving global coordination problems." His conclusion: reinvent everything, from schools to the civil service to the Parliament itself.

But whether their cultural despair was angry or elegiac, whether their nostalgia was restorative or reflective—whether they were *clercs* like Cummings or several steps removed from politics, like Scruton—the nostalgic conservatives laid the groundwork for a

Brexit campaign that felt, to those who supported it, like the last chance to save the country, whatever it took, whatever price had to be paid. Both the "establishment" Conservative Vote Leave campaign, led by Johnson and his Tory colleague Michael Gove, as well as UKIP's own campaign, led by Nigel Farage, told lies. If we left the EU, Johnson claimed, there would be an extra £350 million a week—an imaginary number—for the National Health Service. If we stayed in the EU, we would be forced to accept Turkey as a member, which was also untrue. Farage appeared in front of a poster showing huge crowds of Syrians trekking toward Europe, even though there was no reason why any of them would end up in the United Kingdom, which is not part of the Schengen Area, Europe's border-free zone. In an interview, Cummings later compared this campaign to "Soviet propaganda." But his own campaign also relied on stoking immigration fears and false promises about welfare spending, indeed deliberately linking the two. Among other things, it made a video that claimed, "Turkey is joining the EU. Our schools and hospitals already can't cope." Though it bore no relation to reality, it was viewed 515,000 times.

Once upon a time, the reshaping of ideas into political projects was a matter of writing pamphlets; the Brexit campaign was the end of that idea, and the onset of something new. The Vote Leave campaign cheated, breaking electoral laws in order to spend more money on targeted advertising on Facebook. Animal lovers were shown photographs of Spanish bullfighters; tea drinkers were shown a grasping hand, marked with an EU flag, reaching for a British teacup, alongside an angry slogan: "The European Union wants to kill our cuppa." The Vote Leave campaign used the data stolen by the company Cambridge Analytica to assist with that targeting. All of the Brexit campaigns benefited from Russian trolling operations, though these mostly just echoed what Vote Leave was doing anyway. The atmosphere of the campaign was uglier than any in modern British history. At its height, Jo Cox, a female member of Parliament, was murdered by a man who had become convinced that Brexit meant liberation and "Remain" meant that England would be destroyed by hordes of brown foreigners. Just like the murderer of Paweł Adamowicz, the mayor of Gdańsk, he had been radicalized by the angry rhetoric all around him.

Both then and later, the activists who were bent on restoration of English greatness kept their focus on the goal of leaving. Knowing some of them—and knowing how deeply they care about England, how convinced they are that their civilization is at risk—I understood their frame of mind, even if I didn't agree with it. They believe that the British political system is too corrupt to reform itself, the country has been so transformed as to be unrecognizable, the very essence of the nation is disappearing. But if all of that is true, then only a profound revolution, even a revolution that might alter the very nature of the state—its borders, its traditions, maybe even its democratic institutions—can stop the rot. If Brexit could be that revolution, then anything that led to Brexit, from false spending claims to data manipulation to attacks on the judiciary to Russian money, was acceptable. That prospect of extreme change continued to inspire and motivate them, even when it ran into trouble.

Democracy, in the writings and speeches of some of the Brexiteers, was the paramount reason for Brexit. Back in 2010, Heffer wrote that "Europe has advanced largely by being anti-democratic," that Europe had been "Sovietized," and that Britain needed to escape for the sake of its democracy. Tory MP Michael Gove told an audience in 2016 that "our membership of the EU stops us being able to choose who makes critical decisions which affect all our lives." He hoped, by contrast, that a victory for Brexit would lead to "the democratic liberation of a whole continent." At no point did the Brexiteers seek to achieve their goal without a referendum vote.

But however much they supported democracy in theory, quite a few Brexiteers, especially the ones who worked for the tabloid press, were disgusted by the actual democratic institutions of the United Kingdom in practice. When three British judges ruled, in November 2016, that the British Parliament would have to give its consent before the government could formally withdraw from the EU, the *Daily Mail,* a newspaper run by Brexiteers, ran an extraordinary front page: pictures of the three judges in their wigs and robes and the headline ENEMIES OF THE PEOPLE.

The decision had nothing to do with Brexit. On the contrary, it upheld the sovereignty of Parliament. Nevertheless, the three judges—including the Lord Chief Justice and the Master of the Rolls, to give them their full titles—were excoriated in the accompanying article. Once, these were the sort of establishment figures respected by Burkean conservatives; now they were outsiders, aliens, "out of touch" elites seeking to thwart the "real" Britons. One of them was described, sneeringly, as an "openly gay ex-Olympic fencer." And the judiciary was not the only venerable British institution under assault. Another *Daily Mail* front-page story assaulted the House of Lords under the headline CRUSH THE SABOTEURS.

As the negotiations with the EU dragged on, the Brexiteer scorn for British institutions grew more intense. Inevitably, the process of extracting Britain from forty years of treaties proved far more difficult than the simplistic election slogans had promised. As it turned out, very few of the nostalgic conservatives really understood Europe or European politics, and their predictions about what would happen next were all wrong. Heffer wrote a column arguing that Brexit would lead to a rash of copycat referenda in other European countries; in fact, it led to growing support for the EU. One Tory member of the House of Lords told me just after the vote that he had personally spoken with senior German manufacturers and had been assured that any arrangements made would be favorable to Britain. In fact, the senior German manufacturers started talking about divesting from Britain. During the referendum campaign, nobody had thought at all about Northern Ireland, or the need to build a new British-Irish customs border if Britain were leaving the Single Market. As soon as negotiations began, these immediately emerged as the central issues.

The realization that they had underestimated the costs and overestimated the ease with which Britain could be extracted from Europe led a few Brexiteers to lapse into silence. One journalist told me privately she had changed her mind about Brexit, though I noticed that the tone of her public writings did not change. But others were drawn even more sharply to the idea of chaos. A "no-deal" Brexit—one that meant Britain would crash out of all of its treaties with Europe, leading to an automatic rise in tariffs and legal uncertainty for millions of people—was no longer an unfortunate outcome, to be avoided if at all possible. They wanted disruption. They wanted impact. They wanted *real* change. This, finally, was the moment when it might be possible to convert their nostalgia for a better past into a better future.

There were different versions of this desire for chaos. A sudden drop in economic activity would be good for the nation's soul, some came to believe. Everyone would buck up, tighten their belts, and work harder. "The British are among the worst idlers in the world," a group of pro-Brexit MPs wrote of their countrymen: they needed a shock, a period of hardship, a challenge. This would return Britain—or at least England—to its essence, reveal the country's plucky character. It would force the slothful, decadent modern state to regain, in Johnson's words, "the dynamism of those bearded Victorians."

On the other side of the political spectrum, a different sort of disaster fantasy held sway. The Labour leader, Jeremy Corbyn, hailed from a Marxist tradition that had historically welcomed catastrophe because catastrophe can lead to radical change. Though they never said so in public, Tom Watson, then the deputy leader of the Labour Party, privately told journalist Nick Cohen that a part of the Labour leadership "absolutely believe that if Brexit brings chaos the voters will turn to the radical left." A subset of the British intellectual left also seemed to hope that, at the very least, Brexit would jolt the country out of its capitalist economic system. The left-wing *Jacobin* magazine published an article, for example, arguing that Brexit offers "a once-in-a-lifetime opportunity to show that a radical break with neoliberalism, and with the institutions that support it, is possible."

Still others hoped for a deep crisis, but with a different outcome: that the chaos would lead to a "bonfire of regulations," an abandonment of the welfare state, new opportunities for hedge funds and investors. Britain could become Europe's offshore tax haven, "Singapore-on-Thames," as the Brexit Party MEP Robert Rowland put it to me. Oligarchs would be happy; everyone else would simply have to adjust. Everything would be better.

These were not fringe views, and they were not considered crazy. All these fantasies were expressed by establishment figures: at different times, the prime minister, the leader of the opposition, wealthy financiers. Nobody had voted for that kind of disruption, of course. It was never discussed during the referendum campaign. The majority of Parliament was against it. The majority of the country was against it. But gradually it became, for many Brexiteers, the real goal. And if the institutions of the British state stood in the way, then the institutions would suffer.

I don't think it's coincidental that, at about this time, a few British conservatives—upstanding members of the Tory party, ex-Thatcherites, ex–Cold Warriors— also became enamored of undemocratic polities in other places. Theresa May's government had dropped the old idea that Britain should stand up for democracy around the world with amazing speed; Johnson, during his brief and disastrous tenure as foreign secretary, made no efforts in that direction at all. Britain's only foreign policy interest, after 2016, was Brexit. And so, for example, instead of using its considerable influence in Warsaw to persuade Poland's Law and Justice Party not to pack its courts—the two parties were part of the same caucus in the European Parliament—the Tory party leapt to defend it.

For a few people, this required quite a shift in values. The Tory MEP Daniel Hannan had, for example, been eloquent in his denunciation of Communist lies in the past. Like me, Hannan had even helped Scruton send money to Eastern European dissidents. But he ignored the same kinds of lies when they came from his Law and Justice colleagues in the European Parliament. "I don't want to get into domestic Polish politics," he told me when I asked him about it in January 2020, during his final week in the Strasbourg parliament building.

Some British parliamentarians in Europe went even further. In 2018, MEPs from both the Conservative Party and UKIP voted to protect Orbán from being censured by the EU for illegally undermining the independence of his country's judiciary. Why would politicians from a country dedicated to the rule of law do this? In the words of a former UKIP member of the European Parliament, they wanted to "assert the right of a democratic nation to defy Brussels's interference."

At about the same time, the *Spectator* magazine, my old employer, cheerfully agreed to hold an evening event sponsored by the Századvég Foundation, an institution that loyally promotes the interests of Fidesz, the Hungarian ruling party. The foundation once shut down its own magazine on the grounds that it had published an article critical of the government. "The task of this publication will be to support the government's direction," the editor stated. The topic of the *Spectator*-Századvég event was not press freedom but migrant policy, the subject the Hungarian leadership uses to appeal to anti-immigrant conservatives in Western Europe, even though Hungary itself is not a destination for mass migration and never has been. The event was followed by what was, by all accounts, a jolly drunken evening at the Hungarian embassy at which the ambassador welcomed the British writers and broadcasters around the table as fellow "conservatives," all fighting the same cause.

When I asked the *Spectator*'s editor, Fraser Nelson, about the event, he vehemently denied feeling a shred of sympathy for Hungarian authoritarianism. Though he didn't renounce the association (or, presumably, the sponsorship fee), he did let me write an article arguing that some Brexiteers were "providing intellectual cover for a profoundly corrupt political party, one which will never voluntarily leave the EU because its leaders have invented too many clever ways to hijack EU funds on behalf of their friends." This infuriated the Hungarian ambassador to London, who cornered me at a book party—where he had been invited by another one of my friends—to accuse me of writing something that would make it more difficult to do his job. This accusation was not untrue.

The Hungarians also drew in some people whose anger or disappointment in their own country has led them more actively to seek alternatives elsewhere. One of them was John O'Sullivan—the same John O'Sullivan who was so cavalier about Scotland leaving the United Kingdom—one of Mrs. Thatcher's speechwriters, her ghostwriter, a brilliant stylist, and, in the 1980s and 1990s, the editor of one of the most important American conservative journals, the *National Review*. In that capacity

he once hired my husband as a "roving correspondent";
he came to our wedding. He had a well-deserved reputation as a bon vivant—a mutual friend remembers visiting his apartment and noting that he had nothing in his
refrigerator except a bottle of champagne—and he was
a great talker as well as an excellent writer. But toward
the end of his genuinely distinguished career, O'Sullivan,
then in his seventies, found his way to Budapest.

There he began working for the Danube Institute, a
think tank created and funded, via another foundation,
by the Hungarian government. He described it to me
as "conservative in culture, classically liberal in economics, and Atlanticist in foreign policy." But the Danube
Institute exists, in practice, to make the Hungarian
government presentable to the outside world. It has no
impact inside the country; Hungarian friends describe
its presence in Budapest as "marginal." As a rule,
Hungarians don't read its (admittedly sparse) English-
language publications, and its events are unremarkable
and mostly go unremarked. But O'Sullivan has an office
and a Budapest apartment. He has the means to invite
his many friends and contacts, all conservative writers
and thinkers, to visit him in one of Europe's greatest and
most beautiful cities. I have no doubt that, when they
get there, O'Sullivan is the jovial and witty host that he
always was.

O'Sullivan has defended Orbán many times, including in an introduction to a short book about the Hungarian prime minister. That defense goes, more or less,

like this: Everything you've heard about Hungary is wrong. There is plenty of freedom. Other Europeans criticize Hungary not because of corruption, or because of the government's carefully cultivated xenophobia, but because they dislike Orbán's "Christian" values. This last point appeals strongly to American conservative writers like Christopher Caldwell, who, following O'Sullivan's invitation to Budapest, produced a long article in the *Claremont Review* lauding Orbán's attack on "neutral social structures and a level playing field"—a euphemism for independent courts and the rule of law.

Caldwell also praised the mystical "organic community" that he believes Orbán has created instead. Though only a foreigner would call Orbán's closed, corrupt, one-party state—a world in which the prime minister's friends, family, and cousins get rich, people are promoted and demoted depending on their party loyalty, and everyone else is left out—an "organic community." And only an ideologue could believe that Hungary's European neighbors are annoyed by Orbán's "Christianity." In reality, they are annoyed by the cultivated xenophobia of the anti-Soros and anti-European campaigns, they are annoyed by the legal manipulations that have given the Hungarian prime minister nearly complete control of the press and the electoral process, and they are annoyed by his corruption and use of EU money to fund cronies. In the spring of 2020, they were outraged when Orbán used the coronavirus as an excuse to give his government near-dictatorial powers, including the power to arrest journalists who criticized the government's response to the pandemic. The hypocrisy is infuriating, too: In fact, plenty of non-Europeans and non-Christians—Syrians, Malaysians, Vietnamese—do emigrate to Hungary. They just have to pay.

In 2013, when O'Sullivan first arrived there, the Danube Institute was an eccentric place for someone as distinguished as him to end up. But after the Hungarian government had created a political system in which no opposition party could possibly win; after the state audit office had stripped opposition parties of their campaign funding; after a state holding company had taken control of most of the Hungarian media; after the Hungarian government had forced the Central European University to leave the country; after Orbán's family and friends had enriched themselves on state contracts; after the ruling party had used racism and covert anti-Semitism in its election campaign (Orbán was fighting an unnamed "enemy" who is "crafty" and "international" and "speculates with money"); after Orbán had welcomed a Russian bank with espionage links; after he had undermined U.S. policy in Ukraine; after all that, O'Sullivan's position at the Danube Institute became strange, and the line he sold to visiting friends even more so. By then, the only conceivable reason for the Hungarian government to fund the Danube Institute was to camouflage the true nature of a Hungarian government that was not at all conservative in the old Anglo-Saxon sense, not classically liberal in economics, and not particularly Atlanticist either.

It took me a while to get in touch with O'Sullivan, since he moves around a lot. By the time we managed to speak, over the phone, in the autumn of 2019, he was on a cruise ship, and it was very late his time. We had an unpleasant conversation, though not as unpleasant as the one I'd had with Mária Schmidt. He didn't demand to make his own recording, and he didn't publish an inaccurate version afterward. But he did respond to every question with some version of "whataboutism"—a rhetorical technique once made famous by Soviet officials, in which questions are answered by accusing the questioner of hypocrisy. To my queries about the Hungarian media—90 percent owned and operated by the government or by ruling party–linked companies—he answered that most U.S. media is "more favorable" to the Democratic Party, so the situation is similar. When I asked about the Hungarian government's friendship with Russia, he asked whether Germany was really committed to the United States and NATO. When I asked whether he felt comfortable working for an institution funded by the Hungarian government, he said that "I am absolutely certain that the government in Hungary use policies that I personally don't agree with." But, on the other hand, "there are lots of government policies in different countries that I don't like." When I asked about the Hungarian businessmen threatened by the ruling party, he said that "they should complain about it more."

He agreed that it was interesting and notable that, once upon a time, back in the 1980s, he, Orbán, and I had all been on the same side, and that now we are not. But he thought that was because I had changed, not him. I was now part of a "liberal, judicial, bureaucratic, international elite" that was opposed to "democratically elected parliaments." He didn't really explain how you can even have a "democratically elected parliament" in a state like Hungary, where the government can and does cheat with impunity, where opposition parties can be randomly fined or punished, where a part of the judiciary is politicized, and where the bulk of the media is manipulated by the ruling party. His use of the word *elite* was also curious: in Hungary, the only elite—and it's an overwhelmingly powerful, illiberal, judicial, bureaucratic elite—is the new one that thrives inside Fidesz. It was also curiously unreflective. Once upon a time, O'Sullivan would have been proud to call himself a member of a transatlantic, international elite, one that attended parties with Rupert Murdoch and went to expensive dinners with Conrad Black. But it was late, wherever his cruise ship was. He was annoyed, and so was I.

I don't believe Boris Johnson started out thinking of himself as a member of a new elite, let alone as a revolutionary. He was a certified member of the old elite, after all. And whatever his deputies and advisers believed, he didn't start out being interested in undermining the state, or redefining Britain or England either. He was just trying to win, to be admired; he wanted to go on telling amusing stories and to gain power. But in the new political world created by Brexit, winning required unprecedented steps. The constitution had to be pushed to the limit. The Tory party had to be cleansed of doubters. The rules had to be changed. In the autumn of 2019, he began to change them.

In September 2019, on the advice of Cummings, he took the extraordinary decision to prorogue Parliament—to suspend it, unconventionally and unconstitutionally. He also expelled from the party a group of liberal Tories who were trying to block a "no-deal" Brexit, which was equally unprecedented. Among them were two former chancellors of the exchequer and Churchill's grandson. Some of them, including Dominic Grieve, a former attorney general and one of the last principled pro-European Tories, were actively smeared by the party afterward. An anonymous "Downing Street source"—presumably Cummings—told newspapers that Grieve and others were under investigation for "foreign collusion," language that suggested treason. Johnson refused to deny this absurd story, instead telling a news program, "There is a legitimate question to be asked." Grieve received death threats in the days that followed. Boris also called parliamentary objections to a "no-deal" Brexit a form of "surrender" to the enemy, a comment he tried to pass off as a joke. Not everyone laughed.

On the contrary, some of the people around him were deadly serious. The Brexiteers were furious at Parliament, whose majority fought back with every legal tactic, every parliamentary rule it could muster in order to stop the "no-deal" Brexit that the majority of Britons opposed. Eventually, they agreed to a deal that many had called unacceptable only months before, one that allowed a customs barrier to be placed between Northern Ireland and the rest of the United Kingdom. The "no-deal" scenario had been blocked. But Brexiteers were determined to ensure that nothing could stop them again. The Tory party's manifesto, written in advance of their December 2019 election campaign, contained a hint of the revenge some hoped would be inflicted on those who had used the checks and balances of the constitution so effectively:

> After Brexit we also need to look at the broader aspects of our constitution: the relationship between the government, parliament and the courts; the functioning of the Royal prerogative; the role of the House of Lords; and access to justice for ordinary people.

In the weeks after the election, there were some hints of what might be coming. There were, as in Poland, noises made about undermining public media, perhaps by altering the funding of the BBC. There was, as in Hungary, talk of curtailing or limiting the courts. There was talk of a purge of civil servants too. Cummings advertised that he wanted to hire "misfits and weirdos" to help him make the "large changes in policy and in the structure of decision-making" that would now be necessary. Throughout the divisive referendum campaign and two angry elections, the intellectuals and spin doctors who had thrown their energies behind Brexit had invoked revolution and destruction, the kind of language that hadn't been part of British politics in many years. After Johnson won a commanding majority, a few of them, finally, were in a position to act on it.

They were also suddenly faced with the dilemma laid out by the American statesman Dean Acheson, back in 1962: "Great Britain has lost an empire but not yet found a role." In subsequent decades, Britain had found a role—as one of the most powerful and effective leaders of Europe, as the most important link between Europe and America, as a champion, especially inside Europe, of democracy and the rule of law. Now, in a world dramatically reshaped by a pandemic, Britain's leaders are starting from scratch. Britain's place in the world, its role in the world, even its self-definition—who are the British? what kind of nation is Britain?—is up for grabs once again. In the new landscape created by the double medical and economic crises of 2020—and by Johnson's own dangerous brush with the coronavirus—something very different may emerge.

IV

Cascades of Falsehood

POLITICAL CHANGE—alterations in public mood, sharp shifts in crowd sentiment, the collapse of party allegiance—has long been a subject of intense interest to academics and intellectuals of all kinds. There is a vast literature on revolutions, as well as a mini-genre of formulas designed to predict them. Most of these investigations focus on measurable, quantifiable economic criteria, like degrees of inequality or standards of living. Many seek to predict what level of economic pain—how much starvation, how much poverty—will produce a reaction, force people to the street, persuade them to take risks.

Very recently, this question has become more difficult to answer. In the Western world, the vast majority of people are not starving. They have food and shelter. They are literate. If we describe them as "poor" or "deprived," it is sometimes because they lack things that human beings couldn't dream of a century ago, like air-conditioning or Wi-Fi. In this new world, it may be that big, ideological changes are not caused by bread short-ages but by new kinds of disruptions. These new revolutions may not even look like the old revolutions at all. In a world where most political debate takes place online or on television, you don't need to go out on the street and wave a banner to assert your allegiance. In order to manifest a sharp change in political affiliation, all you have to do is switch channels, turn to a different website every morning, or start following a different group of people on social media.

One of many intriguing aspects of Karen Stenner's research on authoritarian predispositions is that it hints at how and why political revolutions might take place in this new and different twenty-first-century world. Over a crackly video link between Australia and Poland, she reminded me that the "authoritarian predisposition" she has identified is not exactly the same thing as closed-mindedness. It is better described as simple-mindedness: people are often attracted to author-itarian ideas because they are bothered by complexity. They dislike divisiveness. They prefer unity. A sudden onslaught of diversity—diversity of opinions, diversity of experiences—therefore makes them angry. They seek solutions in new political language that makes them feel safer and more secure.

What factors, in the modern world, might provoke people to react against complexity? Some are obvious. Major demographic change—the arrival of immigrants or outsiders—is a form of complexity that has traditionally inflamed that authoritarian impulse, and it still does. It was not a surprise that the migration of hundreds of thousands of people from the Middle East to Europe during the Syrian war of 2016—some arriving at the invitation of the German chancellor, Angela Merkel—inspired a rise in support for political parties in Europe that use authoritarian language and symbols. In some countries, especially those with Mediterranean coastlines, these large numbers really did create a set of genuine problems: how to house and care for people arriving by boat, how to feed them, what to do with them next. Elsewhere in Europe, especially Germany, there were also real issues of housing, training, and assimilation of new immigrants. In some parts of the United States and the United Kingdom, there is evidence that new immigrants create unwelcome competition for some jobs. In many countries there have been serious outbreaks of crime or terrorism directly associated with the newcomers.

But the relationship between real immigrants and anti-immigrant political movements is not always so straightforward. For one, immigration, even from places with a different religion or culture, does not always cause a counterreaction. In the 1990s, Muslim refugees from the wars in former Yugoslavia arrived in Hungary without causing undue distress. Muslim refugees from Chechnya caused no major backlash in Poland either. In recent years, the United States absorbed refugees from Russia, Vietnam, Haiti, and Cuba, among other places, without much debate.

Nor can the backlash against immigrants always be blamed on their failure to assimilate. Anti-Semitism grew strongest in Germany, for example, not when the Jews arrived but precisely when they were integrating, succeeding, even converting. More to the point, it now seems as if a country does not even need to have real immigrants, creating real problems, in order to feel passionately angry about immigration. In Hungary, as Mária Schmidt acknowledged, there are scarcely any foreigners and yet the ruling party has successfully stoked xenophobia. When people say they are angry about "immigration," in other words, they are not always talking about something they have lived and experienced. They are talking about something imaginary, something they fear.

The same point is true of inequality and wage decline, another source of anxiety, anger, and division. Economics alone cannot explain why countries in different business cycles, with different political histories and different class structures—not just Europe and the United States but also India, the Philippines, Brazil—simultaneously developed a similar form of angry politics in 2015 to 2018. "The economy" or "inequality" does not explain why, at that exact moment, everybody got very angry. In a book called *The Totalitarian Temptation,* the French philosopher Jean-François Revel wrote that "capitalism is in deep trouble, no doubt about it. By the end of 1973 its medical report was looking more like a death notice." This diagnosis, made forty years ago, sounds as if it applies to the present. And yet the impact of capitalism's failures was somehow felt in 2016, not 1976.

This is not to say that immigration and economic pain are irrelevant to the current crisis: clearly they are genuine sources of anger, distress, discomfort, and division. But as a complete explanation for political change—as an explanation for the emergence of whole new classes of political actors—they are insufficient. Something else is going on right now, something that is affecting very different democracies, with very different economics and very different demographics, all over the world.

Alongside the revival of nostalgia, the disappointment with meritocracy, and the appeal of conspiracy theories, a part of the answer may lie in the contentious, cantankerous nature of modern discourse itself: the ways in which we now read about, think about, hear, and understand politics. We have long known that in closed societies, the arrival of democracy, with its clashing voices and differing opinions, can be "complex and frightening," as Stenner puts it, for people unaccustomed to public dissent. The noise of argument, the constant hum of disagreement—these can irritate people who prefer to live in a society tied together by a single narrative. The strong preference for unity, at least among a portion of the population, helps explain why numerous liberal or democratic revolutions, from 1789 onward, ended in dictatorships that enjoyed wide support. Isaiah Berlin once wrote of the human need to believe that "somewhere, in the past or in the future, in divine revelation or in the mind of an individual thinker, in the pronouncements of history or science . . . there is a final solution." Berlin observed that not all of the things that human beings think are good or desirable are compatible. Efficiency, liberty, justice, equality, the demands of the individual, and the demands of the group—all these things push us in different directions. And this, Berlin wrote, is unacceptable to many people: "to admit that the fulfilment of some of our ideals may in principle make the fulfilment of others impossible is to say that the notion of total human fulfilment is a formal contradiction, a metaphysical chimera." Nevertheless, unity is a chimera that some will always pursue.

In the more open societies of the West, we have become smug about our tolerance for conflicting points of view. But for much of our recent history, the actual range of those views was limited. Since 1945, the most important arguments have usually unfolded between the center right and the center left. As a result, the range of possible outcomes was narrow, especially in democracies like those in Scandinavia that were most inclined toward consensus. But even in the more raucous democracies, the field of battle was relatively well defined. In the United States, the strictures of the Cold War created bipartisan agreement around U.S. foreign policy. In many European countries, a commitment to the EU was a given. Most of all, the dominance of national television broadcasters—the BBC in Britain, the three networks in the United States—and broad-based newspapers that relied on broad-based advertising revenues meant that in most Western countries, most of the time, there was a single, national debate. Opinions differed, but at least most people were arguing within agreed parameters.

That world has vanished. We now are living through a rapid shift in the way people transmit and receive political information—exactly the sort of communication revolution that has had profound political consequences in the past. All kinds of wonderful things flowed from the invention of the printing press in the fifteenth century: mass literacy, the spread of reliable knowledge, the end of the Catholic Church's monopoly on information. But those same things also contributed to new divisions, to polarization and political change. The new technology made it possible for ordinary people to read the Bible, a change that helped inspire the Protestant Reformation—and, in turn, many decades of bloody religious wars. Martyrs were hanged, churches and villages sacked in a furious, righteous maelstrom that subsided only with the Enlightenment and the broad acceptance of religious tolerance.

The end of religious conflict was the beginning of other kinds of conflicts, between secular ideologies and national groups. Some of these also intensified after another change in the nature of communication: the invention of radio and the end of the monopoly of the printed word. Hitler and Stalin were among the first political leaders to understand how powerful this new medium could be. Democratic governments struggled, at first, to find ways to counter the language of demagogues that now reached people inside their homes. Anticipating how divisive broadcasting might become, the United Kingdom in 1922 created the BBC, which was explicitly designed from the beginning to reach all parts of the country, not only to "inform, educate, entertain" but also to join people together, not in a single set of opinions but in a single national conversation, one that would make democratic debate possible. Different answers were found in the United States, where journalists accepted a regulatory framework, libel laws, licensing rules for radio and television. President Franklin Roosevelt created the fireside chat, a form of communication better suited to the new medium.

Our new communications revolution has been far more rapid than anything we know from the fifteenth century, or even the twentieth. After the printing press was invented, it took many centuries for Europeans to become literate; after radio was invented, newspapers did not collapse. By contrast, the rapid shift in advertising money to Internet companies has, within a decade, severely damaged the ability of both newspapers and broadcasters to collect and present information. Many, though not all, have stopped reporting news altogether; many, though not all, will eventually cease to exist. The most common business model, based on advertising to the general public, meant that they were forced to serve a general public interest and forced to maintain at least a theoretical commitment to objectivity. They could be biased, bland, and boring, but they filtered egregious conspiracy theories out of the debate. They were beholden to courts and regulators. Their journalists conformed to formal and informal ethical codes.

Above all, the old newspapers and broadcasters created the possibility of a single national conversation. In many advanced democracies there is now no common debate, let alone a common narrative. People have always had different opinions. Now they have different facts. At the same time, in an information sphere without authorities—political, cultural, moral—and no trusted sources, there is no easy way to distinguish between conspiracy theories and true stories. False, partisan, and often deliberately misleading narratives now spread in digital wildfires, cascades of falsehood that move too fast for fact checkers to keep up. And even if they could, it no longer matters: a part of the public will never read or see fact-checking websites, and if they do they won't believe them. Dominic Cummings's Vote Leave campaign proved it was possible to lie, repeatedly, and to get away with it.

The issue is not merely one of false stories, incorrect facts, or even election campaigns and spin doctors: the social media algorithms themselves encourage false perceptions of the world. People click on the news they want to hear; Facebook, YouTube, and Google then show them more of whatever it is that they already favor, whether it is a certain brand of soap or a particular form of politics. The algorithms radicalize those who use them too. If you click on perfectly legitimate anti-immigration YouTube sites, for example, these can lead you quickly, in just a few more clicks, to white nationalist sites and then to violent xenophobic sites. Because they have been designed to keep you online, the algorithms also favor emotions, especially anger and fear. And because the sites are addictive, they affect people in ways they don't expect. Anger becomes a habit. Divisiveness becomes normal. Even if social media is not yet the primary news source for all Americans, it already helps shape how politicians and journalists interpret the world and portray it. Polarization has moved from the online world into reality.

The result is a hyper-partisanship that adds to the distrust of "normal" politics, "establishment" politicians, derided "experts," and "mainstream" institutions— including courts, police, civil servants—and no wonder. As polarization increases, the employees of the state are invariably portrayed as having been "captured" by their opponents. It is not an accident that the Law and Justice Party in Poland, the Brexiteers in Britain, and the Trump administration in the United States have launched verbal assaults on civil servants and professional diplomats. It is not an accident that judges and courts are now the object of criticism, scrutiny, and anger in so many other places too. There can be no neutrality in a polarized world because there can be no nonpartisan or apolitical institutions.

The medium of the debate has also changed the

nature of the debate. Advertisements for hair dryers, news about pop stars, stories about the bond market, notes from our friends, and far-right memes arrive in a constant stream on our telephones or computers, each one apparently carrying the same weight and importance. If, in the past, most political conversations took place in a legislative chamber, the columns of a newspaper, a television studio, or a bar, now they often take place online, in a virtual reality where readers and writers feel distant from one another and from the issues they describe, where everyone can be anonymous and no one needs to take responsibility for what they say. Reddit, Twitter, and Facebook have become the perfect medium for irony, parody, and cynical memes: people open them to surf down the screen and be amused. No wonder a plethora of "ironic," "parodic," and "joke" political candidates are suddenly winning elections in countries as disparate as Iceland, Italy, and Serbia. Some are harmless; some are not. A generation of young people now treats elections as an opportunity to show their disdain for democracy by voting for people who don't even pretend to have political views.

This doesn't mean we can or should return to an analog past: there was a lot that was wrong with the old media world, and there is much that is right about the new: political movements, online forums, and new ideas that wouldn't exist without it. But all these changes—from the fragmentation of the public sphere to the absence of a center ground, from the rise of

partisanship to the waning influence of respected neutral institutions—do seem to bother people who have
difficulty with complexity and cacophony. Even if we
weren't living through a period of rapid demographic
change, even if the economy were not in turmoil, even
if there were no health crisis, it is still the case that the
splintering of the center right and the center left, the rise
in some countries of separatist movements, the growth
in angry rhetoric, the proliferation of extremist and racist voices that had been marginalized for half a century
would persuade a chunk of voters to vote for someone
who promises a new and more orderly order.

There are numerous recent examples of how this
works. The destruction of congressional bipartisan-
ship in the United States in the 1990s; the arrival of the
conspiracy-minded Law and Justice Party in the center
of Polish politics in 2005; the Brexit vote in 2016: all
of these polarizing moments radicalized a part of the
population in their respective countries. As Stenner puts
it, "The more the messages conflict with one another,
the angrier these people feel." The Polish novelist Olga
Tokarczuk expressed the same idea in the speech she
gave upon receiving the Nobel Prize in 2019: "Instead
of hearing the harmony of the world, we have heard a
cacophony of sounds, an unbearable static in which we
try, in despair, to pick up on some quieter melody, even
the weakest beat."

Modern democratic institutions, built for an era with
very different information technology, provide little

comfort for those who are angered by the dissonance. Voting, campaigning, the formation of coalitions—all of this seems retrograde in a world where other things happen so quickly. You can press a button on your phone and buy a pair of shoes, but it can take months to form a government coalition in Sweden. You can download a movie at the flick of a wrist, but it takes years to debate a problem in the Canadian Parliament. This is far worse at the international level: multinational institutions like the EU or NATO find it extremely hard to make fast decisions or big changes. Unsurprisingly, people are afraid of the changes technology will bring, and also afraid—with good reason—that their political leaders won't be able to cope with them.

The jangling, dissonant sound of modern politics; the anger on cable television and the evening news; the fast pace of social media; the headlines that clash with one another when we scroll through them; the dullness, by contrast, of the bureaucracy and the courts; all of this has unnerved that part of the population that prefers unity and homogeneity. Democracy itself has always been loud and raucous, but when its rules are followed, it eventually creates consensus. The modern debate does not. Instead, it inspires in some people the desire to forcibly silence the rest.

This new information world also provides a new set of tools and tactics that another generation of *clercs* can use to reach people who want simple language, powerful symbols, clear identities. There is no need, nowadays, to form a street movement in order to appeal to those of an authoritarian predisposition. You can construct one in an office building, sitting in front of a computer. You can test messages and gauge the response. You can set up targeted advertising campaigns. You can build groups of fans on WhatsApp or Telegram. You can cherry-pick the themes of the past that suit the present and tailor them to particular audiences. You can invent memes, create videos, conjure up slogans designed to appeal precisely to the fear and anger caused by this massive international wave of cacophony. You can even start the cacophony and create the chaos yourself, knowing full well that some people will be frightened by it.

It is dawn in the Basque countryside. A man is walking, and then running, in slow motion. He climbs a fence. He crosses a field of wheat while brushing his hands, as in a Hollywood movie, across the tops of the sheaves. All the while, music is playing and a voice is speaking: "If you don't laugh at honor because you don't want to live among traitors . . . if you look toward new horizons without despising your old origins . . . if you can keep your honesty intact in times of corruption . . ."

The sun rises. The man climbs a steep path. He crosses a river. He is caught in a thunderstorm. "If you feel gratitude and pride for those in uniform who protect the wall. . . . If you love your fatherland like you love your parents . . ." The music climaxes, the man is on top of the mountain, the voice finishes: ". . . then you are making Spain great again!" A slogan appears on the screen: *Hacer España Grande Otra Vez.*

The slogan translates as "Make Spain Great Again." The man was Santiago Abascal, and this was an advertisement for Vox. In 2019, Vox was Spain's fastest-growing political party, and Abascal is its leader. In Spanish parliamentary elections three years earlier, Vox and its macho, cinematic Spanish nationalism did not win a single seat. Soon after, one Spanish website posted an article asking, "Why doesn't anybody vote for Santiago Abascal?"

But in the spring of 2019, the party's support went from zero to 10 percent, which earned it twenty-four members in parliament. After another election that autumn—held after the first produced a hung parliament—that number doubled. I visited Madrid several times that year, and the city felt a little bit like London just before the Brexit referendum, or Washington before Trump's election. A lot of the people I met—journalists, academics, publishers—were gloomy about the future. By contrast, the Vox team, a few of whom I also met, had enormous amounts of energy and a clear sense of direction. I had a strong sense of déjà vu: once again, here was a political class about to be hit by an angry wave.

Some of the Spaniards I met were also suffering from déjà vu, though of a different kind: they thought they heard the echoes of the past in Vox's rhetoric. Older Spaniards can still remember the ostentatious nationalism that characterized the dictatorship of Francisco Franco, the chants of *"Arriba España!"* or "Go Spain!" at rallies, the solemn atmosphere of forced patriotism. During most of the four decades that followed the dictator's death in 1975, it seemed as if nobody wanted any of that back. Instead, Spain in the late 1970s went through a transition parallel to the one that Poland and Hungary experienced in the 1990s, joining European institutions, rewriting the constitution, and establishing a national truce. In its way, the democratization of Spain was the postwar world's true proof of concept. The democratization and integration of France, Germany, Italy, and the rest had proved so successful by the time of Franco's death that Spaniards, who had set out on a quite different course after the war, finally clamored to join them.

After the transition was completed, Spain's new democracy was almost ostentatiously consensual. Two main political parties emerged from the old one-party state, and together they agreed to agree. Many former Francoists and their children found their way to the new center-right Popular Party; many former Franco opponents and their children found their way to the new center-left Socialist Party. But both sides arranged tacitly, and sometimes openly, not to talk about the things that had once divided them. Franco was allowed to remain in his elaborate tomb, part of a memorial known as the Valley of the Fallen. His left-wing opponents were allowed to celebrate their own veterans. The civil war that had divided them went undiscussed. The past, seemingly in defiance of Faulkner's famous remark, remained past.

Over the past decade, that consensus has shattered. In response to the economic crisis of 2009, a new far-left party, Podemos, challenged the unity of the center left. In response to corruption allegations on the center right, a liberal party, Ciudadanos—the name means "citizens"— sought to create a new centrist political force. A controversial judicial decision over a rape case brought hundreds of thousands of women onto the streets in big, noisy marches, unsettling many traditional Catholics. A center-left government exhumed Franco's remains, removed them from his elaborate mausoleum, and put them in a cemetery, unsettling Spain's nostalgic conservatives.

Above all, the Catalan secessionist movement challenged the constitutional consensus, and in a visually dramatic manner. Catalonia is a wealthy province, and many of its inhabitants speak Catalan, a separate language; it has a long history of both unity and conflict with the rest of Spain, going back several centuries. Under Franco's dictatorship, any hint of Catalonian separatism was harshly suppressed. By contrast, the Spanish democratic constitution of 1978 gave a good deal of autonomy to all of Spain's regions, allowing regional identities to grow— so much that in 2017, Catalonia's regional government, narrowly controlled by separatists, decided to hold a referendum on independence. The Spanish Constitutional Court declared the referendum illegal. A clear majority of Catalans boycotted the referendum—an emotive event, marred by police brutality—but a majority of those who did vote chose independence.

In the ensuing mayhem, the Spanish Senate imposed direct rule and called new Catalan elections. Some secessionist leaders fled into exile; a dozen others were arrested, put on trial, and eventually given long sentences. When the dust settled, Vox—the only party that gave voice to a loud, strident, antiseparatist Spanish nationalism—was suddenly a player in national politics. Vox took advantage of a law that allowed it to launch a private suit against the Catalan secessionists. The party held a rally in Barcelona, called the Catalan government a "criminal organization," and provoked a demonstration of rock-throwing, barricade-burning, black-masked anarchists in response—an excellent image to rally its supporters. Above all, Vox sought to bring back the feeling of unity that once prevailed at those long-ago *Arriba España!* rallies. And its leaders did so using YouTube, Twitter, Instagram, Telegram, and WhatsApp.

Beginning in the spring of 2018 and continuing through the 2019 election, Abascal kept a tally on Twitter of every rally he held, posting a series of video clips and photographs of bars, conference halls, or eventually stadiums, each one packed to the rafters with people, cheering and clapping. Some of his later tweets also contained the hashtag *#EspañaViva*—#LivingSpain—and rapturous commentary. One example: "Neither death threats from dozens of communists nor insults from television can stop #*EspañaViva*." Some of the most popular rallies were also held under the logo *Cañas por España*—"Beers for Spain." In March 2018, seven hundred tickets to a *Cañas por España* event at a Madrid nightclub sold out in four hours, purchased entirely by people under thirty.

These rallies, and the tweets that described them, as well as the party's constant attacks on the "fake" opinion polls in the "biased" media, had a purpose. They were designed to make anyone following Vox feel as if they were part of something big, exciting, growing—and homogenous. Abascal spoke of a "patriotic movement of salvation of the national union," using grandiose language that also helped Vox's support seem a lot larger than it really was. That was the central pillar of Vox's strategy: use social media to create a feeling of unity around a movement that didn't yet quite exist.

At the same time, Vox found ways of reaching groups of voters who were disgruntled by other aspects of modern life that the mainstream parties weren't addressing. Think about how record companies put together new pop bands: they do market research, they pick the kinds of faces that match, and then they market the band by advertising it to the most favorable demographic. New political parties now operate like that: you can bundle together issues, repackage them, and then market them, using exactly the same kind of targeted messaging—based on exactly the same kind of market research—that you know has worked in other places. The ingredients of Vox were the leftover issues, the ones that others had ignored or underrated, such as opposition to Catalan and Basque separatism; opposition to same-sex marriage; opposition to feminism; opposition to immigration, especially Muslim immigration; anger at corruption; boredom with mainstream politics; plus a handful of issues, such as hunting and gun ownership, that some people care about and others don't; plus a streak of libertarianism, a talent for mockery, and a whiff of restorative nostalgia.

It wasn't an ideology on offer, it was an identity: carefully curated, packaged for easy consumption, cued up and ready to be "boosted" by a viral campaign. All of its slogans spoke of unity, harmony, and tradition. Vox was designed, from the beginning, to appeal to people who were bothered by cacophony. It offered them the opposite.

When I asked Rafael Bardaji about the "Make Spain Great Again" video, he grinned: "That was my idea; it was kind of a joke at the time." Bardaji, a member of Vox since almost the beginning, fits no one's idea of a "far-right" party leader. He is cheerful, bespectacled, and dressed in a suit and tie, just like everyone else in the establishment, center-right world that he comes from. Bardaji was an adviser to the former center-right prime minister José María Aznar, the first really successful Popular Party politician, and he spent much of his early career right in the middle of centrist politics. He is best known for pushing Spain to join the American invasion of Iraq in 2003. According to one famous poll, 91 percent of Spaniards opposed that war. After a group of Islamic jihadis set off explosives at a Madrid train station just a few days before the general election in 2004—nearly two hundred people were killed, and two thousand wounded—Spanish voters blamed Aznar's government for bringing the politics of the Middle East into their country. Unexpectedly, a socialist government was swept into power and the careers of Aznar, and Bardaji, came to an end.

Thanks to his association with that era, Bardaji is perceived as outside the mainstream in Spain. He is frequently referred to as a *neoconservative,* though that word is meaningless in the Spanish context; it just sounds American. He has also acquired a nickname— Darth Vader—which he finds sufficiently amusing to put Darth Vader's picture on his Twitter profile. In Madrid, when I told people I had met him, they raised their eyebrows.

But these definitions—"in the mainstream," "outside the mainstream"—change with time. As it happens, I had met Bardaji back when he was not only an important figure in the Spanish government, but an important figure in what felt, at the time, like a robust, enduring, powerful international alliance. Sometime around 2003 we had dinner in Washington. Bardaji was visiting the American Enterprise Institute, the conservative think tank where my husband was then running a program whose name and goals now seem quaint. This was the New Atlantic Initiative, and it sought, in the wake of the expansion of NATO, to refresh the transatlantic alliance, to bring together "Atlanticist" Europeans and Americans to discuss joint transatlantic goals and projects. Senator John McCain spoke at one New Atlantic Initiative event. Democrats interested in America's role in Europe came too. So did Europeans who cared about America: prominent Tories, enthusiastic Czechs, the occasional Portuguese defense minister. John O'Sullivan was a prominent figure in the Atlanticist world. At the time, someone like Bardaji—an affable, pro-American Spaniard with a strong affinity for Israel—fit right in.

In that era, the transatlantic alliance did not, of course, have quite the same unity of purpose as it had had during the Cold War. There was cooperation in Kuwait and in Bosnia, but no single common enemy, at least not until September 11, 2001. The attack on the World Trade Center galvanized the nations of the West, but unevenly: the French and the Germans joined the war in Afghanistan but not the war in Iraq, for example. Nevertheless, there was a genuine coalition of the willing that wanted to fight Saddam Hussein, including Aznar in Spain, British prime minister Tony Blair, Danish prime minister Anders Fogh Rasmussen, Polish president Alexander Kwasniewski, and a clutch of others. Briefly, it seemed like a coherent group; like Blair, Aznar remains forever marked by it. I met him in 2019 at his office in Madrid and couldn't help but notice the photographs, prominently displayed on the bookshelves, of himself in the Middle East with Blair and George W. Bush, as if pictures from that era marked the most important moment in his long career.

The pictures also seem out of place because Atlanticism—a faith that would have once tied people like O'Sullivan or Aznar closely to a strong international cohort, giving them a clear way of relating to American as well as fellow European conservatives—is no longer an important force, not in Spain and not anywhere else either. People like Aznar already seem to belong to a different world. So, for quite a few years, did Bardaji. During a long decade and a half, he sat on the sidelines and watched a series of Spanish governments come and go, all of them either too far-left or too soft-right for his tastes. If John Major's centrism bored some British conservatives in the years after Thatcher, the center-right Popular Party leaders of the 2010s infuriated some of their most loyal members. Once it returned to power in 2011, the party didn't, as they had hoped it would, stop the growth of the state. It didn't reverse a law on domestic violence that, they believed, unfairly penalizes men. It didn't push back against more publicly critical attitudes to the Franco era either. One Vox member of parliament, Ivan Espinosa, illustrated how he and some of his friends began to feel about Spanish politics by plunking a pair of saltshakers on the table where we were having coffee. "Here," Espinosa said, putting the two shakers together: "This was Spanish politics in the

1980s and 1990s." And "here"—he put a fork down several inches away—is Spain today: "Pulled to the extreme left. Center and the right don't push back. They don't counterattack. They don't have any ideas."

Worst of all, in their view, both the center right and the center left became too accommodating of Basque and Catalan separatism. Abascal—himself the son of a Basque politician who had been threatened by the Basque terrorist group, ETA—as well as Espinosa, Bardaji, and their friends all fumed. But they were out of politics, away from influence, outside the rooms where things happened. During those years, Bardaji started a consultancy; he did some business in Israel and the United States. He worked at Spain's most prominent foreign policy think tank. And then Vox—and Trump—offered him a way back in.

Nor was he alone: the language and tactics of Trump's election suddenly seemed to offer something new to a lot of people who had been on the fringes of politics, not just in America but around the world. Bardaji is not himself an alt-right blogger or a denizen of obscure political chat rooms, but he understood how useful the methods of the American alt-right would be in Spain. They might not capture the majority, but they might win over a significant minority.

They would also annoy a Spanish "establishment" that he believed had drifted to the left, leaving people like him far behind. "Make Spain Great Again," he told me gleefully, "was a kind of provocation. . . . It was just intended to make the left a little bit more angry." The amusement to be had from offending the "establishment"—a classic Breitbartian or Brexiteer sentiment—is the same in Madrid as it is in the United States. Bardaji is an acquaintance of Steve Bannon, with whom he has a mutual friend; they have been photographed together. But Bardaji laughs at the speculation that has created. Spanish journalists, he told me, "give Bannon a relevance that he doesn't have."

The politics of Trump, with his disdain for Europe, for NATO, and for democracy, would have revolted Bardaji in the 1990s. But—like some nostalgic conservatives in Britain—Bardaji had, by 2016, grown tired of "liberal democracy," at least as a slogan and as a unifying idea. As a Spaniard, he told me that he didn't feel he had much in common with a NATO that was gearing up to defend Eastern Europe against Russia. But he did like the idea of joining up with a White House that seemed, at least to start out with, prepared to fight a battle against radical Islam. Though out of the loop in Spain for a decade, he found he had lots of contacts and overlapping interests with the new Trump administration—links that Spain's socialist prime minister did not have. He knew Jason Greenblatt, the Trump administration's first Middle East negotiator. He had long-standing links to the Netanyahu government, which was in turn close to the White House, and got some of Netanyahu's electoral advisers to help Vox. Soon after the U.S. election, he had been in touch with Trump's first national security adviser, Michael Flynn, as well as with Flynn's successor, H. R. McMaster. He had been to Washington to discuss both Trump's first trip to NATO as well as a speech Trump gave in Warsaw in 2017—the speech that, famously, outlined the need to defend the Christian world: "The civilizational aspiration, how the West must defend itself, we were completely in tune on that," Bardaji said.

Although the proportion of actual Spanish Muslims is low—most immigration to Spain is from Latin America—the idea that Christian civilization needs to redefine itself against the Islamic enemy has a special historic echo in Spain. Vox used that echo to its benefit. In one of his videos, Abascal mounted a horse and, like the knights who once fought to reconquer Andalusia from the Arabs, rode across a southern Spanish landscape. Like so many Internet memes, it was serious but unserious: the background music is the theme song from *The Lord of the Rings*.

These links between Vox and the Trump administration suggest not a conspiracy, but common interests and common tactics. They also show how the success of Trump inspired and empowered a group of people who wanted to use a new kind of language in Spain—language designed specifically to appeal to people who feel angered by the Catalan debate, who dislike the way modern discourse has fragmented Spaniards, and who think that social and cultural reform projects have gone too far. In Spain, this is also a group that fears its ideas are in danger of disappearing altogether. Bardaji thinks the polarization of Spanish politics is permanent, and that, for people like himself, it is not just their own political careers, but the nation itself that is at risk. If he and his like-minded friends didn't enter the fray, their cohort, and everything it stood for, could be eliminated from politics. Here is the real source of Vox supporters' fear and anger, and it is genuine. This was the most important thing Bardaji said to me: "We are entering into a period of time when politics is becoming something different, politics is warfare by another means—we don't want to be killed, we have to survive. . . . I think politics now is winner takes all."

Vox is the first post-Franco Spanish political movement deliberately designed to appeal to that part of the population that is unnerved by Spain's polarization. The radicalization of Catalonia will increase its support further. So could feminist protests, angry economic debates, and the return of old historical arguments. So will the presence of Podemos, an openly radical, far-left party in the Spanish government. Vox is a project created by people who understand this. They also know that the party's success will give its creators, its spokesmen, its meme-makers, and its PR companies a new lease on political life—as well as access to a growing network of funders, fans, and Internet trolls with similar ideas, across Europe and beyond.

—

Until very recently, the leaders of "far-right" national-ist or nativist parties in Europe rarely worked together. Unlike center-right Christian Democrats, whose col-laboration created the EU, nationalist parties are rooted in their own particular histories. The modern French radical right has distant origins in the Vichy era. The Italian nationalist right has long featured the intellectual descendants of dictator Benito Mussolini, not to men-tion his actual granddaughter. Law and Justice has its links to the Smolensk plane crash and its own historical obsessions. As a result, attempts to fraternize often foun-dered on old arguments. Relations between the Italian far right and the Austrian far right, for example, once came unstuck after they started arguing, amusingly, over the national identity of South Tyrol, a German-speaking province in northern Italy that has sometimes been Aus-trian. Relations between Vox and Italy's Liga Nord, a nationalist party that started out as a northern Italian separatist movement, grew rocky when Matteo Salvini, the Liga's leader, supported the Catalan separatists.

More recently that has begun to change. Long di-vided by borders and history, some of the intellectuals and ideologues behind these new movements have now found a set of issues they can unite around—issues that work across borders and are easy to sell online. Oppo-sition to immigration, especially Muslim immigration, both real and imagined, is one of them; promotion of a socially conservative, religious worldview is another. Sometimes, opposition to the EU, or to international institutions more generally, is a third. These issues are unrelated—there is no reason why you can't be a pro-European Catholic, as so many have been in the past—and yet those who believe in them have made common cause. Dislike of same-sex marriage, African taxi drivers, or "Eurocrats" is something that even Spaniards and Italians who disagree about their respective separatist movements can share. Avoiding history and old border disputes, they can conduct joint campaigns against the secular, ethnically mixed societies they inhabit, and at the same time appeal to the people who want the raucous debate about these things to come to a halt.

Among those who have tried to understand how this new and poorly understood cross-border campaigning works is a Madrid-based data analytics company called Alto Data Analytics. Alto specializes in applying artificial intelligence to the analysis of data found on Twitter, Facebook, Instagram, YouTube, and elsewhere. In the run-up to the Spanish electoral season, I spent several hours in Madrid, some of them late at night in a restaurant (where else would it be in Spain?) with a friend who works at Alto, and who did not want to be named in this book, or dragged into the Spanish political conversation at all. He showed me a set of elegant, colored network maps of the Spanish online conversation and pointed out the large squiggle in the middle: that was the "mainstream" conversation, in which lots of people were interconnected. He also showed me three outlying, polarized conversations. These were separate echo chambers, whose members were mostly talking and listening to one another. One of them was the Catalan secessionist conversation, another was the far-left conversation, and the third was the Vox conversation.

That was no surprise: these three groups had been building their separate identities for a long time. Nor was it a surprise to learn that my friend had found the largest number of what he called "abnormal, high-activity users" on the Spanish Internet—meaning bots, or else real people who post very frequently and probably professionally—within these three communities. The Vox community accounted for more than half of them. In the spring of 2019, the Institute for Strategic Dialogue (ISD)—a British organization that tracks online extremism—uncovered a network of nearly three thousand "abnormal, high-activity users" that had pumped out nearly 4.5 million pro-Vox and anti-Islamic messages on Twitter in the previous year.

That network's origins were unclear. It had been originally set up to attack the Maduro government of Venezuela. After a terrorist attack in Barcelona in 2017, it switched targets, focusing instead on immigration scare stories, gradually increasing its emotional intensity. Some of the material promoted in the network came originally from extremist networks, and all of it aligned with messages being put out by Vox. On April 22, for example, a week before Spain's polling day, the network was tweeting images of what its members described as a riot in a "Muslim neighborhood in France." In fact, the clip showed a scene from recent antigovernment riots in Algeria.

Both Alto and ISD noticed another oddity. Vox supporters, especially the group identified as abnormal, high-activity users, were very likely to post and tweet content and material from a set of conspiratorial websites, mostly set up at least a year before the 2019 election. These sites, sometimes run by a single person, looked like normal, local news sites but they mixed "ordinary" information with highly partisan articles and headlines that were then systematically pumped into the social media networks. The Alto team found exactly the same kinds of websites in Italy and Brazil in the months before those countries' elections in 2018. In each case, the websites began putting out partisan material—in Italy, about immigration; in Brazil, about corruption and feminism—during the year before the vote. In both countries, they served to feed and amplify partisan themes even before they were really part of mainstream politics. They were not necessarily designed to create false stories. Although some of them do that, their real goal is more sophisticated. They are designed to create false narratives, to repeat themes and to hammer them home, to cherry-pick the news and emphasize particular details, to create anger, annoyance, and fear, over and over again.

In Spain, there were half a dozen such sites, some quite professional and some clearly amateur. Some came from a template. One of the more obscure sites, for example, had exactly the same style and layout as a pro-Bolsonaro Brazilian site, as though both had been designed by the same person, or more likely by the same team of public relations specialists—modern, up-to-date, cutting-edge *clercs*. On the day before the Spanish election, that site's lead story was a familiar conspiracy theory: George Soros would help orchestrate election fraud. Soros had not been a well-known figure in Spain until Vox made him part of the debate. On Vox websites it was possible to find some of the standard conspiracy theories about him; naturally, he was said to be scheming to populate Europe with Muslims.

These kinds of sites are found in many other places as well. The infamous Macedonian websites that sought to influence the U.S. presidential campaign operated along very similar principles. So do the conspiracy sites that belong to the QAnon network. So did the Facebook pages created by Russian military intelligence during the 2016 U.S. election campaign, as well as the clearly identifiable Russian state media sites Sputnik and RT. New versions of this playbook are now being rolled out in the United States as well. In 2019, a Michigan reporter uncovered a network of websites purporting to be local news sites. All of the sites had been set up at the same time, and they all looked like "normal" newspapers with familiar-sounding names: the *Lansing Sun,* the *Ann Arbor Times,* the *Detroit City Wire.* Each contained the same kinds of partisan stories—on how Michiganders support President Trump, for example—mixed in with stories about where to buy the least expensive gasoline. They had been designed, deliberately, to be pumped into hypercharged, conspiratorial, partisan echo chambers.

In recent years, similar kinds of sites have begun to work in concert, across borders, in different languages. In December 2018, the United Nations brought world leaders together to discuss global migration at a low-key summit that produced a dull and nonbinding pact—the Global Compact for Safe, Orderly and Regular Migration. Though the pact received relatively little mainstream media attention, Alto found nearly fifty thousand Twitter users tweeting conspiracy theories about it. Several hundred were doing so in multiple languages, switching between French, German, Italian, and, to a lesser extent, Spanish and Polish. Much like the Spanish network that promotes Vox, these users were taking material from extremist and conspiratorial websites, using identical images, linking to and retweeting one another across borders.

A similar international network went into high gear after the 2019 fire at the Notre Dame Cathedral in Paris. ISD tracked thousands of posts from people claiming to have seen Muslims "celebrating" the fire, as well as from people posting rumors and pictures that purported to prove there had been deliberate arson. A site called CasoAislado had one up almost immediately, claiming that "hundreds of Muslims" were celebrating in Paris and using an image that looked as though people with Arabic surnames were posting smiley-face emoticons under scenes of the fire on Facebook. A few hours later, Abascal tweeted his disgust at these "hundreds of Muslims," using the same image. He linked to it via a post by the American alt-right conspiracy theorist Paul Watson—who, in turn, sourced the same image to a French far-right activist named Damien Rieu. "Islamists want to destroy Europe and Western civilization by celebrating the fire of #NotreDame," wrote Abascal: "Let's take note before it's too late."

These same kinds of memes and images then rippled through Vox's WhatsApp and Telegram fan groups. Members of these groups shared an English-language meme showing Paris "before Macron" with Notre Dame, and "after Macron" with a mosque in its place. They also shared a news video, made about another incident, that seemed to be alluding to arrests and gas bombs found in a nearby car. It was a perfect example of the American alt-right, the European far right, and Vox all messaging the same thing, at the same time, in multiple languages, attempting to create the same emotions across Europe, North America, and beyond.

Slowly, this half-hidden online world is acquiring a real-world face. In an Italian hotel ballroom of spectacular opulence—on red velvet chairs, beneath glittering crystal chandeliers and a stained-glass ceiling—I watched, in the winter of 2020, as some of these new movements tried to join forces. The occasion was a conference held ostensibly in the name of Ronald Reagan and John Paul II, and organized, among others, by John O'Sullivan, whose

Hungarian government–funded institute was listed as a sponsor. There was a through-the-looking-glass feeling about the event, which evoked the names of two men who shared a grand, ambitious, and generous idea of Western political civilization—one in which a democratic Europe and a democratic America would be economically, politically, and culturally integrated—although everyone in the room was dedicated to precisely the opposite vision. The theme of the event was "nationalism," but what really linked those in attendance was a dislike of the societies they inhabit, as well as a genuine fear that some of their own values would soon be lost in them. Speaker after speaker—American, Italian, French, Dutch, British, Polish, Spanish (an MEP from Vox)—got up and described feelings of political persecution, as well as the experience of being a dissident in a world dominated by a set of ideas variously described as "left," "progressive," "enlightenment rational liberal," or even "totalitarian." At times, their distance from political reality was disconcerting. Many mourned the lost idea of "the nation"—and yet there we were, in the center of Rome, where an overtly nationalist, even chauvinist, politician, Matteo Salvini, was just around the corner, leading the race to be the next prime minister.

Still, some of them were very eloquent, even moving. Among the speakers was Marion Maréchal, the charismatic niece of the French far-right leader Marine Le Pen, often mentioned as a future French presidential candidate. Maréchal divided the world into a "we" that included everyone in the room and a "them" that seemed to include everyone from the liberal French president, Emmanuel Macron, to French Stalinists: "We are trying to connect the past to the future, the nation to the world, the family to the society. . . . We represent realism; they are ideology. We believe in memory; they are amnesia." Even as she was saying those words, Macron himself was in Kraków, where he described himself as both a proud Frenchman *and* a proud European. He went on to speak quite a bit more about history and memory that day, as he often does. To Maréchal's fans, this may not matter. Presumably they prefer to hear about history from someone like her, a spokesperson for an ethnic definition of France and Frenchness. Or they may simply share her sense of persecution and are pleased to hear it reflected in public.

Thanks to some rather less eloquent speeches on Polish patriotism and the glories of "sovereignty," the audience in Rome thinned out significantly as the day wore on. But as the final session grew closer, cameramen and journalists began drifting back into the room. When the final speaker entered, he won a standing ovation. This was Viktor Orbán himself, the person, I realized, that many in the room had really come to hear. Not because he was the most well spoken, but because he had achieved some of the things that the others want. Although several speakers had talked about oppressive left-wing ideology at universities, Hungary is the only European country to have shut down an entire university, to have put academic bodies such as the Hungarian Academy of Sciences under direct government control, and to have removed funding from university departments that the ruling party dislikes for political reasons. Although many objected to "left-wing" media, Hungary is also the only European country that has used a combination of political and financial pressure to put most of the private and public media under ruling-party control too. For would-be authoritarian parties and politicians who are still mostly out of power, there was a lot to admire. Hungary is not a big country. But this kind of control, this kind of influence, is what they desire.

Orbán did not make a speech. Instead, he was asked to explain the secrets of his success. With a straight face, Orbán said that it was important not to have to share power with other parties. He did not explain the manipulation, the electoral engineering, and the carefully finessed cheating that had allowed him to maintain his majority. Also, he said, it helps to have the support of the media. In the back of the room where the press was sitting, a few people laughed. The rest of the room nodded, not laughing at all: they sympathized—and they understood.

V

Prairie Fire

WITH OUR POWERFUL founding story, our unusual reverence for our Constitution, our geographic isolation, and our two centuries of relative economic success, modern Americans have long been convinced that liberal democracy, once achieved, was impossible to reverse. The founders themselves were not so certain: their beloved classical authors taught them that history was circular, that human nature was flawed, and that special measures were needed to prevent democracy from sliding back into tyranny. But American history, to most modern Americans, does not feel circular. On the contrary, it is often told as a tale of progress, forward and upward, with the Civil War as a blip in the middle. Cultural despair does not come easily to a nation that believed in the Horatio Alger myth and Manifest Destiny. Pessimism is an alien sentiment in a state whose founding documents, the embodiment of the Enlightenment, contain one of the most optimistic views of the possibilities of human government ever written.

More than that: optimism about the possibilities of government has been coded into our political culture since 1776. In that year it was not at all "self-evident," in most of the world, that all men were created equal. Nor was it obvious, in 1789, that "we the people" were capable of forming a "more perfect union," or even that "we the people" were capable of governing ourselves at all. Nevertheless, a small group of men clustered on the eastern seaboard of what was then a wild continent wrote those words and then built a set of institutions designed to make them come true. They were sanguine about human nature, which they did not believe could be perfected. Instead, they sought to create a system, stuffed with checks and balances, that would encourage people to behave better. Neither then nor later did their lofty words always reflect reality. Neither then nor later did their institutions always function as intended. But over time, the words proved powerful enough and the institutions flexible enough to encompass ever larger circles of fully vested citizens, eventually including not just men but women, people without property or wealth, former slaves, and immigrants from every culture. When the institutions failed, as they sometimes did, the words were recited and repeated in order to persuade people to try again. Abraham Lincoln spoke of America as the "last, best hope of earth." Martin Luther King Jr. dreamed that "one day this nation will rise up and live out the true meaning of its creed: 'We hold these truths to be self-evident; that all men are created equal.'"

From the very beginning, there was also a conviction that this new nation would be different from others. Thomas Jefferson believed that democracy in America would succeed, even when it had failed in France, because the unique history and experiences of Americans had prepared them for it. He thought Americans, "impressed from their cradle" with the belief in democratic self-government, were special precisely because they were isolated from Europe and its cycles of history—"separated from the parent stock & kept from contamination." Others, from de Tocqueville to Reagan, reinterpreted this "exceptionalism" to mean different things. But what really made American patriotism unique, both then and later, was the fact it was never explicitly connected to a single ethnic identity with a single origin in a single space. Reagan's 1989 "shining city on a hill" speech, remembered as the peak moment of "American greatness" and "American exceptionalist" rhetoric, clearly evoked America's founding documents and not American geography or an American race. Reagan called on Americans to unify not around blood and soil but around the Constitution: "As long as we remember our first principles and believe in ourselves, the future will always be ours."

But from the beginning there were also alternatives available, different versions of what America is or should be, different definitions of "the nation." Like a dissonant voice inside a swelling chorus, there have always been groups whose dislike of American ideals ran very deep, reflecting more than mere exhaustion with the government of the day. Since 1776, some have always found the American project naive, frightening, oppressive, or false. Tens of thousands of Loyalists fled to Canada after the Revolution; the Confederate states seceded. For some, disappointment with America was so profound, and rage at America was so intense, that it led them to draw drastic conclusions and take drastic actions.

In the past century and a half, the most despairing, the most apocalyptic visions of American civilization usually came from the left. Inspired by European thinkers and movements—Marxism, anarchism, Bolshevism—the American radicals of the late nineteenth and early twentieth centuries mourned the arrival of a hellish modernity and deplored the failure of American capitalism to ameliorate it. The anarchist Emma Goldman gave voice to a whole class of intellectuals and activists when she wrote in 1917 of what she saw as America's sham institutions: "A free Republic! How a myth will maintain itself, how it will continue to deceive, to dupe, and blind even the comparatively intelligent to its monstrous absurdities."

Goldman was especially disgusted by American military adventures abroad, and by the American patriotic language used to justify them. "What is patriotism?" she asked in an essay published in 1908: Is it "the place of childhood's recollections and hopes, dreams and aspirations?" No, she concluded, it is not:

If that were patriotism, few American men of today could be called upon to be patriotic, since the place of play has been turned into factory, mill, and mine, while deafening sounds of machinery have replaced the music of the birds. Nor can we longer hear the tales of great deeds, for the stories our mothers tell today are but those of sorrow, tears, and grief.

She believed the American dream was a false promise and America itself a place of "sorrow, tears, and grief"— beliefs that led her, initially, to extreme forms of protest. Her comrade and partner, Alexander Berkman, went to prison for a failed attempt to assassinate the industrialist Henry Clay Frick; Berkman was also associated with a failed attempt to bomb the home of John D. Rockefeller Jr. Though she later repudiated violence—and was deeply shocked by the realities of the Bolshevik revolution, once she encountered them—Goldman expressed some understanding, in 1917, for the "modern martyrs who pay for their faith with their blood, and who welcome death with a smile, because they believe, as truly as Christ did, that their martyrdom will redeem humanity."

That kind of language found its way, fifty years later, into the thinking of the Weather Underground. In 1970, this group of radicals threw Molotov cocktails at the home of a New York Supreme Court justice, issued a "Declaration of War" against the United States, and accidentally blew up a Greenwich Village town house while making bombs. Like the anarchists of an earlier era, they had no faith in the American political system or its ability to deliver meaningful change. In their most famous statement, *Prairie Fire,* they wrote of the "deadening ideology of conformism and gradualism," which "pretends to reassure the people" by spreading conciliatory, centrist ideas. This "reformism"—by which they meant the normal activities of democratic politics— "assumes the essential goodness of U.S. society, in conflict with the revolutionary view that the system is rotten to the core and must be overthrown." The Weathermen did not assume the essential goodness of U.S. society. They believed the system was rotten to the core. Sharing Lenin's contempt for elected politicians and legislatures, they were frustrated and bored by the idea of building constituencies or seeking votes.

They were even more angered by the notion of "American exceptionalism," which they denounced, in *Prairie Fire,* by name. In their minds, America could not be special, it could not be considered different, it could not be an exception. The iron laws of Marxism dictated that, sooner or later, the revolution would arrive in America too, bringing to an end America's pernicious influence on the world. Their anger at the very word *exceptionalism* has its echo in the language found in a part of the political left today. The historian Howard Zinn, the author of a history of America that focuses on racism, sexism, and oppression, has gone out of his way to denounce the "myths of American exceptionalism."

Dozens of articles have been published with variations of that same headline in the past two decades. That dislike of America echoes and resonates in endless colloquia and seminars and public meetings, wherever those disappointed with the American idea now gather.

But there is another group of Americans whose disgust with the failures of American democracy has led them to equally radical conclusions, and these also have an echo today. If the left located its gloom in the destructive force of capitalism, the power of racism, and the presence of the U.S. military abroad, the Christian right located its disappointment in what it perceived as the moral depravity, the decadence, the racial mixing, and above all the irreversible secularism of modern America. The writer Michael Gerson, an evangelical Christian as well as an acute, critical analyst of "political" Christianity, has argued that a part of the evangelical community now genuinely believes that America is lost. Gerson, a former George W. Bush speechwriter who is another person now estranged from former colleagues, describes the views of his former friends like this: "A new and better age will not be inaugurated until the Second Coming of Christ, who is the only one capable of cleaning up the mess. No amount of human effort can hasten that day, or ultimately save a doomed world." Until Judgment Day itself, in other words, there is no point in trying to make society better, and indeed it is probably going to get worse. Eric Metaxas, an evangelical talk radio host, argued that a Hillary Clinton victory in 2016 would herald the end of the republic: "The only time we faced an existential struggle like this was in the Civil War and in the Revolution when the nation began." Franklin Graham, the son of evangelist Billy Graham used even more elaborate language during the Obama presidency: "I believe we are in the midnight hour as far as God's clock is concerned or we may be in the last minutes . . . when you see how quickly our country is deteriorating, how quickly the world is deteriorating morally, especially during this administration, we have seen that it has taken like a nosedive off of the moral diving board into just the cesspool of humanity."

This strand of deep right-wing pessimism about America is not entirely new. A version of these same views has been offered to Americans repeatedly, over a period of three decades, by many other speakers and writers, but most famously by Patrick Buchanan. Buchanan is not an evangelical Protestant, but rather a Catholic who shares the same apocalyptic worldview. In 1999, Buchanan announced that he was resigning from the Republican Party and running for the presidency at the head of the Reform Party. In his announcement speech, he lamented the loss of the "popular culture that undergirded the values of faith, family, and country, the idea that we Americans are a people who sacrifice and suffer together, and go forward together, the mutual respect, the sense of limits, the good manners; all are gone." In more recent versions of this lament, he has been more specific about his cultural despair, as he was in the spring of 2016:

> In the popular culture of the '40s and '50s, white men were role models. They were the detectives and cops who ran down gangsters and the heroes who won World War II on the battlefields of Europe and in the islands of the Pacific. The world has been turned upside-down for white children. In our schools the history books have been rewritten and old heroes blotted out, as their statues are taken down and their flags are put away.

Buchanan's pessimism derives partially from his sense of white decline but also, like some of those diametrically opposed to him on the left, from his dislike of American foreign policy. Over the years he has evolved away from ordinary isolationism and toward what seems to be a belief that America's role in the world is pernicious, if not evil. In 2002, he told a television audience, using language that could have equally come from Noam Chomsky or a similar left-wing critic of America, that "9/11 was a direct consequence of the United States meddling in an area of the world where we do not belong and where we are not wanted."

Stranger still, a man who resisted false Soviet narratives for many decades fell hard for a false Russian narrative, created by Putin's political technologists, that Russia is a godly, Christian nation seeking to protect its ethnic identity. Never mind that only a tiny percentage of Russians actually go to church, or that fewer than 5 percent say they have ever read the Bible; never mind that Russia is very much a multiethnic, multilingual state, with a far larger Muslim population than most European countries; never mind that Chechnya, a Russian province, is actually governed by sharia law, or that its government forces women to wear veils and tortures gay men; never mind that many forms of evangelical Christianity are actually banned. The propaganda—the photographs of Putin paying homage to an icon of Our Lady of Kazan, for example, or the incorporation of religious services into his inaugurations—worked on Buchanan, who became convinced that Russia was an ethnic nationalist state of a sort superior to America, which he describes with disgust as a "multicultural, multiethnic, multiracial, multilingual 'universal nation' whose avatar is Barack Obama."

Like those who live on the extreme edges of the American far left, some of those who live on the extreme edges of the far right have long been attracted to violence. There is no need to rehearse here the history of the Ku Klux Klan, to tell the stories of Oklahoma bomber Timothy McVeigh and Charleston shooter Dylann Roof, or to describe the myriad individuals and militia movements who have plotted mass murder, and continue to plot mass murder, in the name of rescuing a fallen nation. In 2017, an Illinois militia set off a bomb at a Minnesota mosque. In 2018, a man who believed Jews were plotting to destroy white America murdered eleven people at a Pittsburgh synagogue. In January 2019, a group of men calling themselves "the Crusaders" plotted to put a bomb in an apartment complex in Garden City, Kansas, because they hoped to murder a large number of Somali refugees. These groups and movements were also inspired by a conviction that democracy is worthless, that elections cannot bring real change, and that only the most extreme and desperate actions can stop the decline of a certain vision of America.

By 2016, some of the arguments of the old Marxist left—their hatred of ordinary, bourgeois politics and their longing for revolutionary change—met and mingled with the Christian right's despair about the future of American democracy. Together, they produced the restorative nostalgic campaign rhetoric of Donald Trump. Two years earlier, Trump had railed against American failure, and called for a solution Trotsky would have appreciated: "You know what solves [this]? When the economy crashes, when the country goes to total hell and everything is a disaster. Then you'll have . . . riots to go back to where we used to be when we were great." Four years before that, his adviser Steve Bannon, who has openly compared himself to Lenin, spoke menacingly of the need for war: "We're gonna have to have some dark days before we get to the blue sky of morning again in America. We are going to have to take some massive pain. Anybody who thinks we don't have to take pain is, I believe, fooling you." In a 2010 speech, he even made a direct reference to the Weathermen, referencing

Prairie Fire and quoting from the Bob Dylan song that gave them their name:

> It doesn't take a weatherman to see which way the wind blows, and the winds blow off the high plains of this country, through the prairie and lighting a fire that will burn all the way to Washington in November.

Trump's inaugural address, written by a team of his advisers—Bannon among them—also contained both left and right strands of anti-Americanism. It included left-wing disgust for the "Establishment," which had "protected itself, but not the citizens of our country": "Their victories have not been your victories; their triumphs have not been your triumphs; and while they celebrated in our nation's capital, there was little to celebrate for struggling families all across our land." It also reflected the evangelical despair about the dire moral state of the nation, "the crime and gangs and drugs that have stolen too many lives and robbed our country of so much unrealized potential."

The inaugural speech did not directly express a longing for a cleansing episode of violence. But the speech on "Western civilization" that Trump delivered in Warsaw a year later, in July 2017—the one Bardaji and his friends helped write—most certainly did. Trump, who seemed surprised by some of what he was reading from the teleprompter ("Think of that!" he marveled at a mention of the Polish origins of Copernicus), was clearly not the author. But the real authors, including Bannon and Stephen Miller, used some of the same language as they had in the inaugural: "The people, not the powerful . . . have always formed the foundation of freedom and the cornerstone of our defense," they wrote, as if Trump himself were not a wealthy, powerful elite businessman who had dodged the draft and let others fight in his place. In a passage describing the Warsaw Uprising—a horrific and destructive battle in which, despite showing great courage, the Polish resistance was crushed by the Nazis— they had Trump declare that "those heroes remind us that the West was saved with the blood of patriots; that each generation must rise up and play their part in its defense." The ominous overtone was hard to miss: "each generation" means that patriots in our generation will have to spill their blood in the coming battle to rescue America from its own decadence and corruption too.

Trump himself contributes new elements to this old story. To the millenarianism of the far right and the revolutionary nihilism of the far left he adds the deep cynicism of someone who has spent years running unsavory business schemes around the world. Trump has no knowledge of the American story and so cannot have any faith in it. He has no understanding of or sympathy for the language of the founders, so he can- not be inspired by it. Since he doesn't believe American democracy is good, he has no interest in an America that aspires to be a model among nations. In a 2017 interview with Bill O'Reilly of Fox News, he expressed his admiration for Vladimir Putin, the Russian dictator, using a classic form of "whataboutism." "But he's a killer," said O'Reilly. "There are a lot of killers. You think our country's so innocent?" Trump replied. Two years earlier, he expressed a similar thought in another television interview, this time with Joe Scarborough. "He's running his country and at least he's a leader," he said of Putin, "unlike what we have in this country. . . . I think our country does plenty of killing also, Joe, so you know."

This way of speaking—"Putin is a killer, but so are we all"—mirrors Putin's own propaganda, which often states, in so many words, "Okay, Russia is corrupt, but so is everyone else." It is an argument for moral equivalence, an argument that undermines faith, hope, and the belief that we can live up to the language of our Constitution. It is also an argument that is useful to the president, because it gives him the license to be a "killer," or to be corrupt, or to break the rules "just like everyone else." On a trip to Dallas I heard a version of this from one of the president's wealthy supporters. Yes, she told me, he is corrupt—but so, she believed, were all of the presidents who went before him. "We just didn't know about it before." That idea gave her—an upstanding citizen, a law-abiding patriot—the license to support a corrupt president. If everybody is corrupt and always has been, then whatever it takes to win is okay.

This, of course, is the argument that anti-American extremists, the groups on the far-right and far-left fringes of society, have always made. American ideals are false, American institutions are fraudulent, American behavior abroad is evil, and the language of the American project—equality, opportunity, justice—is nothing but empty slogans. The real reality, in this conspiratorial view, is that of secretive businessmen, or perhaps "deep state" bureaucrats, who manipulate the voters into going along with their plans, using the cheesy language of Thomas Jefferson as a cover story. Whatever it takes to overthrow these evil schemers is justified. In *Prairie Fire,* the Weather Underground inveighed against "the Justice Department and White House–CIA types." Now Trump does the same. "You look at the corruption at the top of the F.B.I.—it's a disgrace," he told *Fox and Friends* two years into his presidency. "And our Justice Department, which I try and stay away from—but at some point I won't." Later on, he didn't.

This form of moral equivalence—the belief that democracy is no different, at base, from autocracy—is a familiar argument, and one long used by authoritarians. Back in 1986, Jeane Kirkpatrick, a scholar, intellectual, and Reagan's UN ambassador, wrote of the danger both to the United States and to its allies from the rhetoric of moral equivalence that was coming, at that time, from the Soviet Union. Guns, weapons, even nuclear warheads were dangerous to democracies, but not nearly as dangerous as this particular form of cynicism: "To destroy a society," she wrote, "it is first necessary to delegitimize its basic institutions." If you believe that American institutions are no different from their opposite, then there is no reason to defend them. The same is true of transatlantic institutions. To destroy the Atlantic alliance, the community of democracies, she wrote, "it is only necessary to deprive the citizens of democratic societies of a sense of shared moral purpose which underlies common identifications and common efforts."

Trump's victory in 2016 was the victory of exactly this form of moral equivalence. Instead of representing the shining city on the hill, we are no different from the "killers" of Putin's Russia. Instead of a nation that leads "the citizens of democratic societies," we are "America First." Instead of seeing ourselves at the heart of a great international alliance for good, we are indifferent to the fate of other nations, including other nations that share our values. "America has no vital interest in choosing between warring factions whose animosities go back centuries in Eastern Europe," wrote Trump, or his ghostwriter, back in 2000. "Their conflicts are not worth American lives." That's not an indictment of the Iraq War. That's an indictment of America's involvement in the world going back to the beginning of the twentieth century, an indictment of America's involvement in two world wars and the Cold War, a return to the xenophobia and inward-looking isolationism of the 1920s, the era when Trump's father was arrested for rioting with the Ku Klux Klan.

And this is what Trump has proven: beneath the surface of the American consensus, the belief in our founding fathers and the faith in our ideals, there lies another America—Buchanan's America, Trump's America—one that sees no important distinction between democracy and dictatorship. This America feels no attachment to other democracies; this America is not "exceptional." This America has no special democratic spirit of the kind Jefferson described. The unity of this America is created by white skin, a certain idea of Christianity, and an attachment to land that will be surrounded and defended by a wall. This America's ethnic nationalism resembles the old-fashioned ethnic nationalism of older European nations. This America's cultural despair resembles their cultural despair.

The surprise is not that this definition of America is there: it has always existed. The surprise is that it emerged in the political party that has most ostentatiously used flags, banners, patriotic symbols, and parades to signify its identity. For the party of Reagan to become the party of Trump—for Republicans to abandon American idealism and to adopt, instead, the rhetoric of despair—a sea change had to take place, not just among the party's voters, but among the party's *clercs*.

"It was cocktail hour on the opening day of the new, Republican-dominated Congress, and the long, chandelier-lighted parlor of David Brock's town house in Georgetown was filling up with exuberant young conservatives fresh from events on the Hill." That was the opening sentence, in 1995, of a *New York Times Maga-zine* cover story called "The Counter Counterculture." The author was the late James Atlas, and one by one, he introduced a series of characters. There was young David Brooks, then of *The Wall Street Journal* editorial page. There was Brock himself, best known at the time for his vicious investigations into the personal affairs of President Bill Clinton. There were my friends David Frum—he is described as "a former *Wall Street Journal* editorial writer"—and his wife Danielle Crittenden, with whom, years later, I cowrote my Polish cookbook.

There are amusing details—expensive Georgetown restaurants where educated conservative elites pour scorn upon educated liberal elites—but the tone is not negative. A parade of other names and short profiles follows: Bill Kristol, John Podhoretz, Roger Kimball, Dinesh D'Souza. I knew most of them at the time the article appeared. I was then working in London for the *Spectator,* and my relationship to this group was that of a foreign cousin who visited from time to time, inspired mild interest inside the family, but never quite made it to the inner circle. I wrote occasionally for the *Weekly Standard,* edited by Kristol; for the *New Criterion,* edited by Kimball; and once for the *Independent Women's Quarterly,* then edited by, among others, Crittenden. I also knew, slightly, a woman whose appearance, in a leopard-skin miniskirt, was the most notable thing about the magazine's cover photograph: Laura Ingraham, who had been a clerk to Supreme Court justice Clarence

Thomas and was then an attorney at a tony law firm. In the penultimate paragraph Atlas finds himself, near midnight, "careering through the streets of downtown Washington with Brock in Ingraham's military-green Land Rover at 60 miles an hour looking for an open bar while the music of Buckwheat Zydeco blasted over the stereo."

Ingraham occasionally reconfirms, on her television programs or in public speeches, the main thing I associated her with at the time: a devotion to Reagan and Reaganism, the same devotion that would have been shared, at that time, by all of those people at Brock's cocktail party. Or perhaps devotion to Reagan is a bit too specific. What really held that group together—and what drew me to it as well—was a kind of post–Cold War optimism, a belief that "we had won," that the democratic revolution would now continue, that more good things would follow the collapse of the Soviet Union— the same optimism we had in Poland at that time, and that I remember so well from New Year's Eve of 1999. This wasn't the nostalgic conservatism of the English; this was something more buoyant, more American, an optimistic conservatism that wasn't backward-looking at all. Although there were darker versions, at its best it was energetic, reformist, and generous, predicated on faith in the United States, belief in the greatness of American democracy, and ambition to share that democracy with the rest of the world.

But that moment turned out to be briefer than we

expected. If the end of the Cold War and Thatcherism produced dissatisfaction among British conservatives, in America the end of the Cold War produced deep divisions and unresolvable quarrels. Before 1989, American anti-Communists—ranging from centrist Democrats all the way through the outer edges of the Republican Party—had been tied together by their determination to oppose the Soviet Union. But the group was not monolithic. Some were Cold Warriors because, as realpolitik diplomats or thinkers, they feared the traditional Russian aggression lurking beneath Soviet propaganda, they worried about nuclear war, and they cared about American influence around the world. Others—and I include myself in this category—thought that we were fighting against totalitarianism and dictatorship, and for political freedom and human rights. Still others, it turns out, fought the Soviet Union because Soviet ideology was explicitly atheist and because they believed that America stood on the side of God. When the Soviet Union fell apart, the links that had held these different anti-Communists together broke as well.

The tectonic shift did take time. Its scope and scale were not immediately obvious. The events of 9/11 probably held the group together for far longer than would have otherwise been the case. But in the end, the evening at Brock's house turned out to be yet another party whose attendees now no longer speak to one another. Only two years after it took place, Brock himself, in an article entitled "Confessions of a Right-Wing Hit Man," recanted, accusing the right of "intellectual intolerance and smug groupthink." Brooks slowly drifted to the center and became a *New York Times* columnist who writes books about how to live a meaningful life. Frum became a speechwriter for George W. Bush, then became disillusioned with the party's xenophobic and conspiratorial fringe, then broke away completely after the election of Donald Trump. Kristol followed the same trajectory a little bit later. Others—D'Souza, Kimball—went in precisely the opposite direction.

My own break came in 2008, thanks to the ascent of Sarah Palin, a proto-Trump, and the Bush administration's use of torture in Iraq. I even wrote an article, "Why I Can't Vote for John McCain," explaining how I thought the party had changed. (On rereading, I find this article was mostly dedicated to praising McCain. Still, McCain, who had made a wonderful speech at the Washington launch of my book *Gulag: A History,* never spoke to me again.) But it was not until Donald Trump became the party's candidate that I learned how different my understanding of the world had become from some of my American friends. That little group of "young conservatives" broke cleanly in half.

In 2017, Sam Tanenhaus wrote another article about a party, this time in *Esquire* magazine. This was the party that the Frums gave at their house in Washington to mark the publication of my book *Red Famine: Stalin's War on Ukraine,* a party that contained a large contingent of what Tanenhaus described as "a cadre of the uprooted and displaced, writers, intellectuals, and pundits who, had they gathered in Paris or London—well, Ottawa, anyway—might have worn the haunted glamour of émigrés and exiles." Tanenhaus gently mocked this gathering of "Never Trumpers," among other things laughing at the "Eastern Europe–themed hors d'oeuvres" served at a party to celebrate the publication of a book about a famine, which was fair enough. But he also made a serious point: "For many of the guests . . . the rise of Trump changed the old refrain 'It can happen here' into something more dire and pressing: 'It's happening now and must be stopped.'"

Not all of our old acquaintances felt the same way—and indeed, they were not invited. The guest lists drawn up by my friends in the 1990s and the ones created by those same friends in the late 2010s were very different. For one, there were a handful of center-left Democrats in the room, people whom the Frums did not know thirty years earlier. There were also some absences. Roger Kimball, for example, was not there. Back in 1992, Kimball actually wrote an appreciation of *La trahison des clercs,* parts of which later appeared as an introduction to a new English-language edition of Benda's famous book. In that 1992 essay, he noted with approval that Benda—"writing at a moment when ethnic and nationalistic hatreds were beginning to tear Europe asunder"—opposed partisanship and believed in "the ideal of disinterestedness, the universality of truth." At that moment in time, perhaps because "ethnic and nationalist hatreds" were on the rise in Yugoslavia and the former Soviet Union, the ideal of intellectual neutrality seemed to Kimball worth celebrating.

By 2019, Kimball had himself become the very opposite of disinterested; nor was he any longer particularly attached to the "universality of truth." During the impeachment hearings of 2019, he produced a string of articles for a pro-Trump website called American Greatness, repeatedly mocking or ignoring the evidence, never really contested by the president's lawyers, that President Trump had broken the law. The 1992 Kimball wrote that "the disintegration of faith in reason and common humanity leads not only to a destruction of standards, but also involves a crisis of courage." The 2019 Kimball compared Democratic members of Congress to "that angry mob which sided with Barabbas in front of Pontius Pilate"—a statement that implicitly equates Trump with Jesus. He never mentioned the cowardice of Republican senators who, with the exception of Mitt Romney, were afraid to acknowledge that the president had used the instruments of American foreign policy for his personal benefit. The "crisis in courage" was right there, sitting in front of him. Kimball was no longer able to see it.

Ingraham was not there either, though in an earlier era I would have been glad to have her at a party marking the publication of a book about Soviet crimes, and she would have been delighted to come. But since the 1990s, our trajectories had gone in radically different directions. She left the law, drifted into the world of conservative media, tried for a long time to get her own television show. Though these early attempts all failed, she eventually had a popular talk radio program. I was a guest on the program a couple of times, once after the Russian invasion of the nation of Georgia in 2008. Listening again to the conversation—the magic of the Internet ensures that no sound bite is ever lost—I was struck by how consistent it was with the optimistic conservatism of the 1990s. Ingraham was still talking about America's power to do good, America's ability to push back against the Russian threat. But she was already groping for something else. At one point, she quoted from an article by Pat Buchanan, one of her mentors, who had repeatedly railed against the pointlessness of any American relationship with Georgia, an aspiring democracy, and lauded Russia, a country he imagined to be more "Christian" than his own.

The reference was a hint at some other changes. For at some point her Reaganite optimism disappeared and slowly hardened into the apocalyptic pessimism shared by so many others. This can be found in much of what she says and writes nowadays: America is doomed, Europe is doomed, Western civilization is doomed. Immigration, political correctness, transgenderism, the culture, the establishment, the left, the "Dems" are responsible. Some of what she sees is real: so-called "cancel culture" on the Internet, the extremism that sometimes flares up on university campuses, the exaggerated claims of those who practice identity politics are a political and cultural problem that will require real bravery to fight. But it is no longer clear that she thinks these forms of left-wing extremism can be fought using normal democratic politics. In 2019, she had Buchanan himself on her show and put the point to him directly: "Is Western civilization, as we understood it, actually hanging in the balance? I think you could actually make a very strong argument that it is tipping over the cliff." Like Buchanan she has also become doubtful about whether America could or should play any role in the world. And no wonder: If America is not exceptional but degenerate, why would you expect it to achieve anything outside its borders?

The same sense of doom colors her views of immigration. For many years now Ingraham has, like so many others in the Fox universe, depicted illegal immigrants as thieves and murderers, despite overwhelming evidence that immigrants commit fewer crimes overall than native-born Americans. Nor is this a familiar, reasonable call for more restrictions at the border. She has also called on President Trump to end not just illegal immigration but also legal immigration, referring more than once to the "massive demographic changes" in America, "changes that none of us ever voted for, and most of us don't like." In some parts of the country, she said, "it does seem like the America that we know and love doesn't exist anymore." She finished by addressing Trump directly:

This is a national emergency, and he must demand that Congress act now. There is something slipping away in this country, and it's not about race or ethnicity. It's what was once a common understanding by both parties that American citizenship is a privilege, and one that at a minimum requires respect for the rule of law and loyalty to our constitution.

And if the real America, the true America, is disappearing, then extreme measures might be required to save it. In 2019, Ingraham nodded along when one of her guests, the conservative lawyer Joseph diGenova, began to speak of the coming cultural conflict in America: "The suggestion that there's ever going to be civil discourse in this country for the foreseeable future is over . . . it's going to be total war," he said: "I do two things, I vote and I buy guns." When Rafael Bardaji said that "we don't want to be killed, we have to survive," he was speaking metaphorically. Ingraham promotes a group of Americans who believe that politics may soon be real warfare, with real violence.

That dark pessimism, with its echoes of the most alarmist, the most radical left- and right-wing movements in American political history, helps explain how Ingraham became, long before many others, a convinced supporter of Donald Trump. She has known Trump since the 1990s; they once went on a date, though apparently that didn't go well—she found him pompous ("He needs two separate cars, one for himself and one for his hair," she told some mutual friends). Nevertheless, she was an early supporter of his involvement in politics, even allowing him to rant about birtherism on her show. She spoke on his behalf at the Republican convention, arguing his case even before the rest of her party would go along. She has had special access to him throughout his presidency and is one of several people at Fox who speak to him regularly.

Her belief in him, or at least his cause, profoundly shaped Ingraham's coverage of the coronavirus pandemic in the spring of 2020. Like her fellow Fox News broadcasters, she at first downplayed the story, blaming Democrats for hyping the virus, calling it "a new pathway for hitting President Trump." Later, she engaged in active disinformation, ignoring medical experts and heavily promoting the drug hydroxychloroquine before it had been tested; she mentioned it three days before Trump began to promote it himself. In April, she also joined the president's strange campaign against his administration's own lockdown policies, encouraging "rebels" to rise up against the quarantine. One of her tweets gave away some of her deeper views: "How many of those who urged our govt to help liberate the Iraqis, Syrians, Kurds, Afghanis, etc., are as committed now to liberating Virginia, Minnesota, California, etc?" The use of the word *liberation,* the direct equivalence drawn between Saddam Hussein, a man who carried out mass murders, and the democratically elected American governors, who were trying to keep their citizens safe from an epidemic—these were not the thoughts of someone who has faith in American democracy.

A few elements of Ingraham's trajectory remain mysterious. One is her frequent invocation of moral values, Christian values, personal values. During a 2007 speech, she told a group in Dallas that "without virtue there is no America. Without virtue we will be ruled by tyrants." She then made a list of those virtues: "honor, courage, selflessness, sacrifice, hard work, personal responsibility, respect for elders, respect for the vulnerable." None of these virtues can be ascribed to Donald Trump. More complicated is her participation in the opprobrium the president heaps on all immigrants, and her own fears that legal immigration has undermined "the America we know and love." Ingraham herself has three adopted children—all immigrants.

I don't know how she explains these contradictions to herself, because Ingraham wouldn't speak to me. Like my friend Ania Bielecka, she answered one email and then went silent. But there are clues. Some mutual friends point out that she is a convert to Catholicism, and a breast cancer survivor who is deeply religious: she told one of them that "the only man who never disappointed me was Jesus." The willpower she required to survive in the cutthroat world of right-wing media—especially at Fox News, where female stars were often pressured to sleep with their bosses—should not be underestimated. This combination of personal experiences gives a messianic edge to some of her public remarks. In that same 2007 speech, she spoke about her religious conversion. If it weren't for her faith, she said, "I wouldn't be here . . . I probably wouldn't be alive." That was why, she said, she fought to save America from the godless: "If we lose faith in God, as a country—we lose our country."

Professional ambition, the oldest excuse in the world, is part of the story too. Partly thanks to Trump, and her connection to Trump, Ingraham finally got her own prime-time Fox television show, with a vast salary to match. She has secured interviews with him at key moments, during which she poses only flattering questions. "By the way, congratulations on your polling numbers," she told him while interviewing him on the anniversary of D-Day. But I don't think, for someone as intelligent as Ingraham, this is the full explanation. She ran a radio show throughout the many years in which Fox didn't give her a television program, and I believe she will go back to running a radio show if they ever cancel her program. As in the case of so many biographies, picking apart the personal and the political is a fool's game.

There are some clues to her thinking from other times and other places. Perhaps personal contradictions—like having a gay son and supporting a homophobic party, as my Polish friend does, or damning immigration while adopting children from abroad—actually *feeds* extremism, or anyway the use of extremist language. The Polish writer Jacek Trzynadel has described what it felt like, in

Stalinist Poland, to be a loud advocate for the regime and to feel doubt about it at the same time. "I was shouting from a tribune at some university meeting in Wrocław, and simultaneously felt panicked at the thought of myself shouting. . . . I told myself I was trying to convince [the crowd] by shouting, but in reality I was trying to convince myself." For some people, loud advocacy of Trump helps to cover up the deep doubt and even shame they feel about their support for Trump. It's not enough to express tepid approval of a president who is corrupting the White House and destroying America's alliances. You have to shout if you want to convince yourself as well as others. You have to exaggerate your feelings if you are to make them believable.

But the answer may also lie, simply, in the depth of Ingraham's despair. The America of the present is a dark, nightmarish place where God speaks to only a tiny number of people; where idealism is dead; where civil war and violence are approaching; where democratically elected politicians are no better than foreign dictators and mass murderers; where the "elite" is wallowing in decadence, disarray, death. The America of the present, as she sees it, and so many others see it, is a place where universities teach people to hate their country, where victims are more celebrated than heroes, where older values have been discarded. Any price should be paid, any crime should be forgiven, any outrage should be ignored if that's what it takes to get the real America, the old America, back.

VI

The Unending of History

PROFOUND POLITICAL SHIFTS like the one we are now living through—events that suddenly split families and friends, cut across social classes, and dramatically rearrange alliances—have happened before. Not nearly enough attention has been paid in recent years to a late-nineteenth-century French controversy that prefigured many of the debates of the twentieth century—a controversy that holds a mirror up to the arguments of the twenty-first century too.

The Dreyfus affair was triggered in 1894 when a traitor was discovered in the French army: somebody had been passing information to Germany, which had defeated France a quarter century earlier and still occupied the formerly French province of Alsace-Lorraine. French military intelligence investigated and claimed that it had found the culprit. Captain Alfred Dreyfus was Alsatian, spoke with a German accent, and was a Jew—and therefore, in the eyes of some, not a real

Frenchman. As it would turn out, he was also innocent. The real spy was Major Ferdinand Esterhazy, another officer who would, several years later, resign his commission and flee the country.

But French army investigators created fake evidence and gave false testimony. Dreyfus was court-martialed, found guilty, and subjected to public humiliation. In front of a huge, jeering crowd on the Champ de Mars, an adjutant ripped the officer's stripes off his uniform and broke his sword. Dreyfus shouted back: "You are degrading an innocent man! Long live France! Long live the army!" Afterward, he was sent into solitary confinement on Devil's Island, off the coast of French Guiana.

The ensuing controversy—Romain Rolland called it a "combat between two worlds"—divided French society along lines that suddenly seem familiar. Those who maintained Dreyfus's guilt were the alt-right—or the Law and Justice Party, or the National Front, or indeed the QAnon cultists—of their time. Using the screaming headlines of France's yellow press, the nineteenth-century version of a far-right trolling operation, they knowingly pushed a conspiracy theory. They printed posters with snakes emerging from Dreyfus's head—an old anti-Semitic trope—and cartoons depicting him as an animal with a broken tail, racist "memes" in an era before that term was in use. Their leaders lied to uphold the honor of the army. Their adherents clung to their belief in Dreyfus's guilt—and their absolute loyalty to the nation—even when the fakery was revealed.

To persuade them to maintain this loyalty, a whole claque of nineteenth-century *clercs* had to drop their commitment to objective truth. Dreyfus was not a spy. To prove that he was, the anti-Dreyfusards had to disparage evidence, law, justice, and even rational thought. Like Langbehn, the German writer who idolized Rembrandt, they eventually attacked science itself, because it was modern and universal, and because it came into conflict with the emotional cult of ancestry and place. "In every scientific work," wrote one anti-Dreyfusard, there is something "precarious" and "contingent." They also attacked the characters, the personalities, the legitimacy, and the patriotism of the people who defended Dreyfus. Such people were "idiots" and "foreigners," people not fit to be citizens of France.

The anti-Dreyfusards called themselves the "true French"—the true elite, as opposed to the "foreign" and disloyal elite. One of their leaders, Edouard Drumont, created a newspaper, *La Libre Parole*—"Free Speech"—that was both anticapitalist and anti-Semitic, anticipating some of the nationalist-socialist authoritarians of the twentieth century and indeed of our own day. He accused the Jews of plotting to destroy the French army, French power, and France herself.

The Dreyfusards, meanwhile, argued that some principles are higher than loyalty to national institutions, and that it did indeed matter whether Dreyfus was guilty or not. Above all, they argued, the French state had an obligation to treat all citizens equally, whatever their religion. They too were patriots, but of a different sort. They conceived of the nation not as an ethnic clan but as the embodiment of a set of ideals: justice, honesty, objectivity, the neutrality of the courts. Theirs was a more cerebral patriotism, more abstract and harder to grasp, but not without an appeal of its own. In his famously passionate essay "J'accuse," published in 1898, Emile Zola declared that he bore no personal animosity toward the men who had fabricated the case against Dreyfus. Instead, he wrote, "to me, they are only entities, spirits of social evil. And the act I am hereby accomplishing is only a revolutionary means to hasten the explosion of truth and justice."

Those two visions of the nation, this disagreement about "who we are," split France right down the middle—or, perhaps, revealed a split that had been there all along, beneath the placid assumptions of rapidly industrializing, modernizing France. Tempers flared. Social allegiances changed—and guest lists were altered. In the later volumes of his great novel *Remembrance of Things Past,* Marcel Proust described how the Dreyfus case ruined friendships and reorganized society. One fashionable lady in his story becomes anti-Dreyfusard in order to gain entry into aristocratic salons whose members consider her "doubly meritorious" because she is married to a Jew. Another, seeking to curry favor with a Dreyfusard hostess, "declared that all of the people in her world were idiots." A famous cartoon by the satirist Caran d'Ache shows a French family eating dinner. In the first scene, they all sit politely. In the second scene they are fighting, struggling, throwing food, smashing furniture. The caption explains, "They had begun to speak of it"—meaning the Dreyfus case. Leon Blum, France's first Jewish prime minister, remembered the arguments as "no less violent than the French Revolution or World War I."

In the end, the Dreyfusards won. Dreyfus was finally brought home in 1899. He was formally pardoned in 1906. In that same year, Georges Clemenceau, the publisher of Zola's "J'accuse," became prime minister of France. In one of the passages at the very end of Proust's novel, his narrator returns from the provinces after a long illness and discovers that no one is talking about Dreyfus—"this name had been forgotten"—and all of the alliances have shifted once again.

But victory was not permanent. In the early twentieth century, an anti-Dreyfusard backlash once again gained force. Students in Paris began to reject the outcome of the Dreyfus affair. Instead, they adopted an ostentatiously "conservative outlook," as the historian Tom Conner has described it, "based on traditional values such as family, Church and nation." In 1908—the same year that Emma Goldman questioned the very existence of American patriotism—the proto-fascist Action Française movement, founded by a prominent anti-Dreyfusard, Charles Maurras, organized a hate campaign against a historian, Amédée Thalamas. Maurras—Benda lists him as one of the *clercs*—was angered because Thalamas had dared suggest that Joan of Arc's religious visions might have been mere auditory hallucinations instead of sacred signs from God. A gang of activists attacked Thalamas during one of his lectures at the Sorbonne and forced him into hiding. Maurras eventually aligned himself with the Vichy regime that collaborated with Hitler after 1940— using, of course, the slogan "France First."

The political wheel turned again. Hitler was defeated, Vichy was ejected. Maurras was tried and convicted as a traitor. Upon hearing the verdict, he exclaimed, more than half a century after the famous scene on Champ du Mars, *"C'est la revanche de Dreyfus!"*: "It's the revenge of Dreyfus."

Since the war, a different vision of France, one based on rational thought, rule of law, and integration with Europe, has held sway. But the spirit of the *clercs* who sought to smear Dreyfus, to join Vichy, and to fight for France First lives on. Marine Le Pen's "France for the French" nationalism, with its evocation of ancient native symbols and heroes—above all, Joan of Arc— and Marion Maréchal's social conservatism are now pitted against Emmanuel Macron's broader vision of a Republican France that still stands for a set of abstract values, among them impartial justice and the rule of law. Sometimes the struggle becomes violent. When the *gilets jaunes*—yellow-jacketed, anti-establishment anarchists—rioted in Paris in the spring of 2019, they smashed a statue of Marianne, the female symbol of the Republic, the embodiment of the abstract state.

The Dreyfus affair was sparked by a single cause célèbre. Just one court case—one disputed trial—exposed unresolvable divisions between people who had previously not really been aware that they disagreed with one another, or at least had not been aware that it mattered. Two decades ago, different understandings of "Poland" must already have been present, just waiting to be exacerbated by chance, circumstance, and personal ambition. Before Trump's election, different definitions of what it means to be "American" were on offer as well. Even though we fought a civil war that struck powerfully against the nativist, ethnic definition of what it means to be an American, it lived on long enough to be reincarnated in 2016. The Brexit vote and the chaotic debates that followed are proof that some older ideas about England and Englishness, long submerged into a broader definition of "Britain," also retain a powerful appeal. The sudden surge of support for Vox is a sign that Spanish nationalism did not disappear with Franco's death. It merely went into hibernation.

All of these debates, whether in 1890s France or 1990s Poland, have at their core the questions that lie at the center of this book: How is a nation defined? Who gets to define it? Who are *we*? For a long time, we have imagined that such questions were settled—but why should they ever be?

—

In August 2019, we threw a party. This time the party was in the summer and so there was sunbathing on the grass and swimming in the pond instead of snow and sleigh rides. Instead of fireworks, we organized a bonfire. But it was not just the weather: Poland's success—its economic, political, and cultural success—also made things different from New Year's Eve of 1999. This time, a company run by a local friend, the owner of a profitable bakery chain, organized the food, which was far superior to the vats of beef stew we'd made twenty years earlier. Another friend, a former member of parliament from our region who happens to play electric guitar, asked some of his friends to perform, and so there was live music instead of cassette tapes. Some guests stayed at the new hotels in Nakło nad Notecią, the nearby town, one of them a former brewery beautifully converted by a local businessman as a kind of labor of love. Once again I kept lists of who was sleeping where, but the whole thing was much easier, because all kinds of things that had been unthinkable luxuries in 1989 or even 1999—things like portable sound systems or balsamic vinegar—are widely available now, in use at a thousand Polish parties and weddings every weekend.

Some of the guests were familiar. One friend who came from New York in 1999 returned in 2019, this time with his husband and son. A Polish couple came without the children who had themselves grown up and married. The group that came from Warsaw included a few fellow refugees from what used to be the "right," as well as some we wouldn't have dreamed of inviting twenty years earlier, people who had then belonged to what used to be called the "left." In the intervening years we lost some friends, but we also made new ones.

There were others, too, including neighbors from the village, the mayors of some nearby towns, and, again, a small group of friends from abroad, flying in from Houston, London, Istanbul. At one point, I noticed the local forest ranger engaged in heated discussion with the former Swedish foreign minister, Carl Bildt, with whom my husband created the Eastern Partnership between the EU and Ukraine several years earlier. At another point, I saw a well-known lawyer, the grandson of a notorious Polish nationalist of the 1930s, engrossed in conversation with a London-based friend who was born in Ghana. In the previous two decades, the world had shrunk sufficiently for all of them to meet one another in the same rural Polish garden.

I also noted that the false and exaggerated division of the world into "Somewheres" and "Anywheres"—people who are supposedly rooted to a single place versus people who travel; people who are supposedly "provincial" versus those who are supposedly "cosmopolitan"—had completely broken down. At our party, it was simply not possible to tell who belonged to which category. People who live in our obscure piece of Polish countryside were delighted to speak to people who do not. As it turned out, people with fundamentally different backgrounds could get along just fine, because most people's "identities" stretch beyond this simple duality. It is possible to be rooted to a place and yet open to the world. It is possible to care about the local and the global at the same time.

One group of guests hadn't been born at all, or had only recently been born, in 1999. These were our sons' friends from school and university, an eclectic mix of Poles, other Europeans, and Americans—from Warsaw, Bydgoszcz, Connecticut, and south London. They arrived by train and slept on floors or in one case in an outdoor hammock. They swam in the lake, slept late the next morning, and then swam in the lake again. They mixed English and Polish, danced to the same music, knew the same songs. No deep cultural differences, no profound civilizational clashes, no unbridgeable identity gaps appeared to divide them.

Maybe the teenagers who feel both Polish and European, who don't mind whether they are in the city or the country, are harbingers of something else, something better, something that we can't yet imagine. Certainly there are many others like them, and in many countries. I've recently met Zuzana Čaputová, for example, the new president of Slovakia, an environmental lawyer from a small town who won a national election by knitting together—just like Vox—a coalition of people who care about disparate things: the environment, corruption, police reform. I was also lucky enough to meet Agon Maliqi, a young Kosovar who promotes liberal ideas and democratic culture through art, film, and education. "What the West experienced as decades of struggle came to us as a piece of paper," he told me. His goal is to make the ideas written down on that piece of paper seem real to ordinary people. I did a podcast with Flavia Kleiner, a Swiss history student who got tired of her country's version of restorative nostalgia and decided to push back against it. She and some of her friends declared themselves "the children of 1848"—descendants of Switzerland's liberal revolution—and began promoting a different sort of patriotism, online and offline, and helped defeat some nationalist referendums. Europe, America, and the world are full of people—urban and rural, cosmopolitan and provincial—who have creative and interesting ideas about how to live in a world that is both more fair and more open.

They have many hurdles to overcome. In the spring of 2020, as the new coronavirus spread across Europe and around the world, their global optimism—any global optimism—suddenly looked naive. On March 13— Friday the thirteenth, as it happened—my husband was driving down a Polish highway when he turned on the news and learned that the country's borders would shut down in twenty-four hours. He pulled over and called me. I bought a ticket from London to Warsaw minutes later. The following morning, Heathrow Airport was spookily empty except for the Warsaw flight, which was packed with people trying to get one of the last commercial trips back into their country. During check-in, agents were refusing to board passengers without a

Polish passport (I have one) or residency documents. Then someone realized that the new rules went into effect only at midnight, and so I witnessed a conversation between one of the stewards and two non-Polish passengers: "You realize that you might not be able to fly out again. You realize that you may be in Warsaw for a very long time. . . ."

That same day, we called our college freshman son in the United States and told him to get to the airport. He had been planning to stay with friends and family after his university closed. Instead, we gave him thirty minutes' notice to get onto one of the last flights to London, connecting to one of the last flights to Berlin. By the time he landed in Europe on Sunday, Poland had shut its borders to all public transportation. He took a train from Berlin to the town of Frankfurt an der Oder, at the Polish-German border. Then he got out and walked across the bridge that spans the border, carrying his luggage, as if in a Cold War movie about a spy exchange. He saw roadblocks, soldiers with guns, men in hazmat suits taking temperatures, drones in the air, marveling, among other things, because he'd never seen a border in continental Europe before. My husband picked him up on the other side. Our other son remained on the other side of the Atlantic, stuck for many weeks.

The Polish government's seemingly unplanned decision to close the border caused massive chaos. Polish citizens were stranded all over the place, and the government was forced to arrange charter flights to get them

home. Thousands of citizens of Ukraine, Belarus, and
the Baltic states—including truck drivers and tourists
just trying to get home—were lined up in their cars at
the Polish-German border for several days, using nearby
fields as a toilet, because border guards were refusing
non-Poles entry. The German Red Cross was handing
out drinks, food, and blankets. None of these harsh,
dramatic measures stopped the virus: the epidemic
had already begun to spread, and continued spreading,
even after the borders were shut. Polish hospitals were
quickly overwhelmed, not least because the rhetoric
of the nationalist government had persuaded so many
educated doctors to leave the country in the previous
five years. But despite the chaos—perhaps even because
of the chaos—the border clampdown was immensely
popular. The state was *doing* something. And this may
be a harbinger of what is to come.

Throughout history, pandemics have led to an expansion of the power of the state: at times when people
fear death, they go along with measures that they believe, rightly or wrongly, will save them—even if that
means a loss of freedom. In Britain, Italy, Germany,
France, the United States, and many other places, there
was a consensus that people needed to stay home, that
quarantines needed to be enforced, that police needed
to play an exceptional role. But in a few places, fear of
disease became, alongside the other unsettling aspects of
modernity, inspiration for a whole new generation of authoritarian nationalists. Nigel Farage, Laura Ingraham,

Mária Schmidt, and Jacek Kurski, along with the trolls who work for Vox in Spain or the alt-right in America, had already prepared the intellectual ground for that kind of change—and so it came to pass. At the end of March, Viktor Orbán in Hungary enacted a law allowing himself to rule by decree and allowing his government to arrest journalists and jail them for five years for criticizing official efforts to fight the virus. There was no need for these measures, and they did not help the Hungarian hospitals that were also overburdened, as in Poland, by lack of investment and emigration. The point was to use the measures to shut down debate. Opposition politicians who objected were jeered by the state media as "pro-virus."

It might be a turning point. Maybe my children and their friends—all of our friends, and all of us, really, who want to go on living in a world where we can say what we think with confidence, where rational debate is possible, where knowledge and expertise are respected, where borders can be crossed with ease—represent one of history's many cul-de-sacs. We may be doomed, like glittering, multiethnic Habsburg Vienna or creative, decadent Weimar Berlin, to be swept away into irrelevance. It is possible that we are already living through the twilight of democracy; that our civilization may already be heading for anarchy or tyranny, as the ancient philosophers and America's founders once feared; that a new generation of *clercs,* the advocates of illiberal or authoritarian ideas, will come to power in the twenty-first century, just as they did in the twentieth; that their visions of the world, born of resentment, anger, or deep, messianic dreams, could triumph. Maybe new information technology will continue to undermine consensus, divide people further, and increase polarization until only violence can determine who rules. Maybe fear of disease will create fear of freedom.

Or maybe the coronavirus will inspire a new sense of global solidarity. Maybe we will renew and modernize our institutions. Maybe international cooperation will expand after the entire world has had the same set of experiences at the same time: lockdown, quarantine, fear of infection, fear of death. Maybe scientists around the world will find new ways to collaborate, above and beyond politics. Maybe the reality of illness and death will teach people to be suspicious of hucksters, liars, and purveyors of disinformation.

Maddeningly, we have to accept that both futures are possible. No political victory is ever permanent, no definition of "the nation" is guaranteed to last, and no elite of any kind, whether so-called "populist" or so-called "liberal" or so-called "aristocratic," rules forever. The history of ancient Egypt looks, from a great distance in time, like a monotonous story of interchangeable pharaohs. But on closer examination, it includes periods of cultural lightness and eras of despotic gloom. Our history will someday look that way too.

I began with Julian Benda, a Frenchman who, writing in the 1920s, anticipated the turbulence to come. Let me end with an Italian who, writing in the 1950s, had already lived through more than a lifetime's worth of turbulence. The novelist Ignazio Silone was exactly the age that I am now when he wrote "The Choice of Comrades," an essay in which he tried to describe, among other things, why he was still engaged in politics, despite so many disappointments and defeats. Silone had joined and left the Communist Party; he may, some believe, have first collaborated with fascism before rejecting that too. He had lived through wars and revolutions, had been under illusions and then been disillusioned, had written as both an anti-Communist and antifascist. He had seen the excesses of two different kinds of extremist politics. Still, he thought the struggle was worth continuing. Not because there was a nirvana to be obtained, and not because there was a perfect society to be built, but because apathy was so deadening, so mind-numbing, so soul-destroying.

He was also living in an era when people lived, as they do today, with both the far right and the far left, with different kinds of extremists all shouting at the same time. Many of his compatriots reacted by declaring that "all politicians are crooks" or "all journalists lie" or "you can't believe anything." In postwar Italy, this form of skepticism, anti-politics, and whatever-ism had even acquired a name, *qualunquismo*. Silone had seen the impact. "Political regimes come and go," he wrote, but "bad habits remain"—and the worst habit is nihilism, "a disease of the spirit which can be diagnosed only by those who are immune from it or have been cured of it, but to which most people are quite oblivious, since they think it corresponds to a perfectly natural mode of being: 'That's how it has always been; that's how it will always be.'"

Silone does not offer a panacea or a miraculous antidote because there isn't one. There is no final solution, no theory that will explain everything. There is no road map to a better society, no didactic ideology, no rule book. All we can do is choose our allies and our friends—our comrades, as he puts it—with great care, for only with them, together, is it possible to avoid the temptations of the different forms of authoritarianism once again on offer. Because all authoritarianisms divide, polarize, and separate people into warring camps, the fight against them requires new coalitions. Together we can make old and misunderstood words like *liberalism* mean something again; together we can fight back against lies and liars; together we can rethink what democracy should look like in a digital age.

Like refugees struggling to reach a distant goal on a dark path we are forced, Silone writes, to pick our way through the night without any clear idea of whether we will arrive: "The clear, ancient Mediterranean sky, once filled with shining constellations, is overcast; but this small circle of light that remains to us enables us at least to see where to place our feet for the next step."

I feel lucky to have spent so much time with people who care what happens after we take that next step.

To some, the precariousness of the current moment seems frightening, and yet this uncertainty has always been there. The liberalism of John Stuart Mill, Thomas Jefferson, or Václav Havel never promised anything permanent. The checks and balances of Western constitutional democracies never guaranteed stability. Liberal democracies always demanded things from citizens: participation, argument, effort, struggle. They always required some tolerance for cacophony and chaos, as well as some willingness to push back at the people who create cacophony and chaos.

They always acknowledged the possibility of failure— a failure that would change plans, alter lives, break up families. We always knew, or should have known, that history could once again reach into our private lives and rearrange them. We always knew, or should have known, that alternative visions of our nations would try to draw us in. But maybe, picking our way through the darkness, we will find that together we can resist them.

Acknowledgments

Christian Caryl, Danielle Crittenden, David Frum, Cullen Murphy, Cristina Odone, Peter Pomerantsev, Alexander Sikorski, Radek Sikorski, Christina Hoff Sommers, Jacob Weisberg, and Leon Wieseltier all read drafts or draft chapters of this book, for which I am extremely grateful. Jeff Goldberg commissioned the article for *The Atlantic* that inspired this book, and Scott Stossel, Denise Wills, and the rest of the editing team at *The Atlantic* helped shape my thinking about it. Fred Hiatt and Jackson Diehl of *The Washington Post* editorial page sent me to Spain to research and report what became the Spanish part of this book; more importantly, many of the other ideas here were first explored in columns I wrote for *The Washington Post* over the past two decades.

This is now the fourth book put together with the same transatlantic editing team: Stuart Proffitt in London, Kristine Puopolo in New York, and the same agent, the legendary Georges Borchardt. All were extremely patient with this, a very different project from the previous ones, and I appreciate their dedication. Many thanks to Maryanne Warrick for help putting together the endnotes, and to Daniel Meyer, Nora Reichard, and Alice Skinner for help with production and copyediting.

Notes

1 *New Year's Eve*

7 a documentary called *Invasion:* "Kulisy, cele, metody, pieniądze. Jak działa inwazja LGBT," TVPINFO, October 10, 2019, https://www.tvp.info/44779437/kulisy-cele -metody-pieniadze-jak-dziala-inwazja-lgbt.

7 gave a sermon describing homosexuals: Marek Jędraszewski, archbishop of Krakow, quoted in Filip Mazurczak, "Krakow's Archbishop Jędraszewski under Fire for Remarks about 'Rainbow Plague,'" *Catholic World Report,* August 16, 2019, https:// www.catholicworldreport.com/2019/08/16/krakows-archbishop -jedraszewski-under-fire-for-remarks-about-rainbow-plague/.

9 each time postulating a different explanation: investigative films include "Pierwszy film śledczy o tragedii smoleńskie," April 10, 2010, https://www.youtube.com/watch?v= _RjaBrqoLmw; "Magazyn śledczy Anity Gargas," TVP, March 29, 2018, https://vod.tvp.pl/video/magazyn-sledczy -anity-gargas,29032018,36323634; "Jak 8 lat po katastrofie wygląda Smoleńsk?," TVPINFO, April 5, 2018, https://www .tvp.info/36677837/jak-8-lat-po-katastrofie-wyglada-smolensk -magazyn-sledczy-anity-gargas; "Magazyn śledczy Anity Gargas," TVP, February 27, 2020, https://vod.tvp.pl/video/ magazyn-sledczy-anity-gargas,27022020,46542067.

9 as "scabby" and "greedy": Rafal Ziemkiewicz,

Twitter post, https://twitter.com/R_A_Ziemkiewicz/status/
637584669115072512?2=20.

9 "blackmailers": Rafal Ziemkiewicz, *Fakty Interia,* April 13,
2018, https://fakty.interia.pl/opinie/ziemkiewicz/news-czy
-izrael-jest-glupi,nId,2568878.

9 regrets his former support for Israel: Rafal Ziemkiewicz, *Wir-
tualne Media,* February 2, 2018, https://www.wirtualnemedia
.pl/artykul/rafal-ziemkiewicz-nie-mam-powodu-przepraszac
-za-parchow-i-zydowskie-obozy-zaglady-marcin-wolski-dal
-sie-podejsc.

11 *wSieci* cover: June 2016, https://wiadomosci.gazeta.pl
/wiadomosci/1,114883,20191010,na-okladce-wprost-jasniejaca
-twarz-lewandowskiego-czyli-jak.html.

11 *Do Rzeczy* cover: September 5, 2016, http://www.publio.pl
/tygodnik-do-rzeczy,p147348.html.

11 fired from a job that I didn't have: The think tank later cor-
rected the story but TVP never took the story down. TVP,
September 21, 2016, https://www.tvp.info/27026877/think-tank
-w-waszyngtonie-po-tym-artykule-zwolnil-pania-applebaum
-ze-wspolpracy.

12 "Is friendship possible": Mihail Sebastian, *Journal 1935–1944:
The Fascist Years* (Lanham, MD: Rowman & Littlefield, 2012).

12 "No, you're wrong": Mihail Sebastian, *For Two Thousand Years,*
trans. Philip Ó Ceallaigh (New York: Other Press, 2017).

14 "false and braggart words": Plato, *Republic,* ed. and trans.
C. J. Emlyn-Jones and William Preddy (Cambridge, MA:
Harvard University Press, 2013).

14 "talents for low intrigue": Alexander Hamilton, John Jay, and
James Madison, *The Federalist Papers,* no. 68.

15 "without any other social ties": Hannah Arendt, *The Origins of
Totalitarianism* (London: Penguin Classics, 2017).

16 authoritarian predisposition: Author interview with Karen
Stenner, July 19, 2019.

17 his 1927 book *La trahison des clercs:* Julien Benda, *The Betrayal
of the Intellectuals* [*La trahison des clercs*] (Boston: Beacon Press,
1955).

11 *How Demagogues Win*

24 "invariably replaces all first-rate talents": Hannah Arendt, *The Origins of Totalitarianism* (London: Penguin Classics, 2017).

24 freedom of the press "is a deception": Vladimir Lenin, "Draft Resolution on Freedom of the Press," *Pravda,* November 7, 1932, https://www.marxists.org/ar.chive/lenin/works/1917/nov /04.htm.

24 "hollow phrase": Vladimir Lenin, speech at the opening session of the First Congress of the Communist International, March 2, 1919, https://www.marxists.org/archive/lenin/works /1919/mar/comintern.htm.

24 "a machine for the suppression": Lenin, speech given to the first Congress of the Communist International, March 14, 1919.

27 "better sort of Pole": "Kaczyński krytykuje donosicieli. Gorszy sort Polaków," YouTube, December 16, 2015, https://www .youtube.com/watch?v=SKFgVD2KGXw.

31 "I saw what doing politics was really about": Author interview with Jarosław Kurski, April 2, 2016.

32 "a person who wants to be on top": Author interview with anonymous source, April 4, 2016.

34 "The ignorant peasants will buy it": Jacek Kurski, quoted in Agnieszka Kublik, "Kłamczuszek Jacek Kurski," *Wyborcza .pl,* May 19, 2015, https://wyborcza.pl/politykaekstra/1,132907 ,17946914,Klamczuszek_Jacek_Kurski.html.

34 "without scruples": Author interview with Senator Bogdan Borusewicz, April 6, 2016.

36 The clip shows Schetyna pausing and frowning: reprinted in "'Ordynarna manipulacja' TVP Info," *Wiadomosci,* April 21, 2018, https://wiadomosci.wp.pl/czy-oni-ludzi-naprawde-maja -za-durni-ordynarna-manipulacja-tvp-info- 6243821849708161a.

43 "You destroyed him": Jan Cienski, "Polish President Bucks Ruling Party over Judicial Reforms: During a Bad-Tempered Debate, Jarosław Kaczyński Accuses the Opposition of 'Murdering' His Brother," *Politico,* July 18, 2017, https://www

.politico.eu/article/polish-president-bucks-ruling-party-over
-judicial-reforms/.

49 so-called "mercenaries of Soros": Pablo Gorondi,
Associated Press, April 12, 2018, https://apnews.com
/6fc8ca916bdf4598857f58ec4af198b2/Hungary:-Pro-govt
-weekly-prints-list-of-%27Soros-mercenaries%27.

49 Schmidt agreed to speak with me: Author interview with
Mária Schmidt, November 14, 2017.

50 "post-colonial" mindset: Ivan Krastev and Stephen Holmes,
"How Liberalism Became 'the God That Failed' in Eastern Europe," *Guardian,* October 24, 2019, https://www
.theguardian.com/world/2019/oct/24/western-liberalism-failed
-post-communist-eastern-europe.

52 institutions of "bourgeois democracy": Vladimir Lenin,
"Working Class and Bourgeois Democracy," *Vperyod* 11, no. 3
(January 24, 1905), https://www.marxists.org/archive/lenin
/works/1905/jan/24.htm.

54 Though Barrès "began as an intellectual skeptic": Julien
Benda, *The Betrayal of the Intellectuals* [*La trahison des clercs*]
(Boston: Beacon Press, 1955).

III *The Future of Nostalgia*

56 "The post-1989 liberal moment": Author conversation with
Stathis Kalyvas, June 21, 2018.

60 "A shriller note could now be heard": Evelyn Waugh, *Decline
and Fall* (London: Chapman & Hall, 1928).

62 "I was sort of chucking these rocks": Boris Johnson, interview
with Sue Lawley, *Desert Island Discs,* BBC, November 4, 2005,
https://www.bbc.co.uk/programmes/p00935b6.

66 "We are Greeks to their Romans": Geoffrey Wheatcroft,
"Not-So-Special Relationship: Dean Acheson and the Myth
of Anglo-American Unity," *Spectator,* January 5, 2013, https://
www.spectator.co.uk/2013/01/not-so-special-relationship/.

67 Graham Greene's novel: Graham Greene, *The Quiet American*
(Melbourne: Heinemann, 1955).

68 "I'm so isolated, I'm like Colonel Kurtz": Boris Johnson as

quoted in James Pickford and George Parker, "Does Boris Johnson Want to Be Prime Minister?," *Financial Times,* September 27, 2013, https://www.ft.com/content/f5b6a84a-263c-11e3-8ef6-00144feab7de.

70   "culture of freedom, openness, and tolerance": From Boris Johnson, "Athenian Civilisation: The Glory That Endures," speech at the Legatum Institute, September 4, 2014, https://www.youtube.com/watch?v=qeSjF2nNEHw.

70   "Brexit will be crushed": Lizzy Buchan, "Boris Johnson 'Thought Brexit Would Lose, but Wanted to Be Romantic, Patriotic Hero,' says David Cameron," *Independent,* September 16, 2019, https://www.independent.co.uk/news/uk/politics/boris-johnson-brexit-david-cameron-leave-remain-vote-support-a9107296.html.

73   "reflective" nostalgia of the émigré: Svetlana Boym, *The Future of Nostalgia* (New York: Basic Books, 2016).

75   "cultural despair": Fritz Stern, *The Politics of Cultural Despair: A Study in the Rise of the Germanic Ideology* (Berkeley: University of California Press, 1961).

76   "It has gradually become an open secret": Julius Langbehn, *Rembrandt as Educator* (London: Wermod and Wermod Publishing Group, 2018).

79   Thatcher's most important pupil: Charles Moore, *Margaret Thatcher, The Authorized Biography, Vol. 3: Herself Alone* (London: Penguin Books, 2019).

80   "thanks to a happy accident of birth": Simon Heffer, "The Sooner the 1960s Are Over, the Better," *Telegraph,* January 7, 2006, https://www.telegraph.co.uk/comment/personal-view/3622149/Simon-Heffer-on-Saturday.html.

81   "the slightest scintilla of principle": Simon Heffer, "David Cameron Is Likely to Win, but Don't Expect a Conservative Government," *Telegraph,* July 28, 2009, https://www.telegraph.co.uk/comment/columnists/simonheffer/5926966/David-Cameron-is-likely-to-win-but-dont-expect-a-Conservative-government.html.

81   called Cameron a "liar": Simon Heffer, "David Cameron's Disgraceful Dishonesty over the EU Is Turning Britain

into a Banana Republic," *Telegraph,* May 21, 2016, https://www.telegraph.co.uk/opinion/2016/05/21/david-camerons-disgraceful-dishonesty-over-the-eu-is-turning-bri/.

82 "pay a personal tribute to the civilization": Roger Scruton, *England: An Elegy* (London: Pimlico, 2001).

84 compared Britain's EU membership to "appeasement": William Cash, interview with Simon Walters, "Tory MP and Son of a War Hero Compares Current Situation to Pre-War Europe and Warns Britain Is Heading for Appeasement," *Daily Mail,* February 13, 2016, https://www.dailymail.co.uk/news/article-3446036/Tory-MP-son-war-hero-compares-current-situation-pre-war-Europe-warns-Britain-heading-APPEASEMENT.html.

85 "a foreign power overruling": Simon Heffer, "The EU Empire Is Going to Fail. On Thursday, We Can Protect Britain from the Chaos of Its Death Throes," *Telegraph,* June 19, 2016, https://www.telegraph.co.uk/news/2016/06/19/the-eu-empire-is-going-to-fail-on-thursday-we-can-protect-britai/.

87 "systemic dysfunction of our institutions": Dominic Cummings, "On the Referendum #33: High Performance Government, 'Cognitive Technologies,' Michael Nielsen, Bret Victor, & 'Seeing Rooms,'" *Dominic Cummings's Blog,* June 26, 2019, https://dominiccummings.com/2019/06/26/on-the-referendum-33-high-performance-government-cognitive-technologies-michael-nielsen-bret-victor-seeing-rooms/.

87 "old institutions like the UN": Cummings, "On the Referendum #33."

88 "Soviet propaganda": Bagehot, "An Interview with Dominic Cummings," *Economist,* January 21, 2016, https://www.economist.com/bagehots-notebook/2016/01/21/an-interview-with-dominic-cummings.

90 "Europe has advanced largely": Simon Heffer, "The Collapse of the Euro Would Open the Door to Democracy," *Telegraph,* May 25, 2010, https://www.telegraph.co.uk/comment/columnists/simonheffer/7765275/The-collapse-of-the-euro-would-open-the-door-to-democracy.html.

90 "our membership of the EU stops us": "Brexit Brief: Dreaming of Sovereignty," *Economist,* March 19, 2016, https://www .economist.com/britain/2016/03/19/dreaming-of-sovereignty.

91 ENEMIES OF THE PEOPLE: Cover, *Daily Mail,* November 3, 2016.

91 "openly gay ex-Olympic fencer": James Slack, "Enemies of the People: Fury over 'Out of Touch' Judges Who Have 'Declared War on Democracy' by Defying 17.4m Brexit Voters and Who Could Trigger Constitutional Crisis," *Daily Mail,* November 3, 2016, https://www.dailymail.co.uk/news/article-3903436 /Enemies-people-Fury-touch-judges-defied-17-4m-Brexit -voters-trigger-constitutional-crisis.html.

91 CRUSH THE SABOTEURS: Cover, *Daily Mail,* April 19, 2017, https://www.dailymail.co.uk/debate/article-4427192/DAILY -MAIL-COMMENT-saboteurs-simmer-down.html.

91 copycat referenda: Simon Heffer, "The EU Empire Is Going to Fail. On Thursday, We Can Protect Britain from the Chaos of Its Death Throes," *Telegraph,* June 19, 2016, https://www .telegraph.co.uk/news/2016/06/19/the-eu-empire-is-going-to -fail-on-thursday-we-can-protect-britai/.

92 "among the worst idlers": "British Workers 'Among Worst Idlers,' Suggest Tory MPs," BBC, August 18, 2020, https:// www.bbc.com/news/uk-politics-19300051.

93 "dynamism of those bearded Victorians": Boris Johnson, "The Rest of the World Believes in Britain. It's Time That We Did Too," *Telegraph,* July 15, 2018, https://www.telegraph.co.uk /politics/2018/07/15/rest-world-believes-britain-time-did/.

93 "believe that if Brexit brings chaos": Author interview with Nick Cohen, March 2020; Nick Cohen, "Why Are Labour's Leaders So Quiet on Europe? Maybe It's the Lure of Disaster?," *Guardian,* December 16, 2018, https://www.theguardian .com/commentisfree/2018/dec/16/why-are-labour-party-leaders -so-quiet-on-europe---maybe-it-is-the-lure-of-disaster.

93 "once-in-a-lifetime opportunity": Thomas Fazi and William Mitchell, "Why the Left Should Embrace Brexit," *Jacobin,* April 29, 2018, https://www.jacobinmag.com/2018/04/brexit -labour-party-socialist-left-corbyn.

96 "providing intellectual cover": Anne Applebaum, "How Viktor Orbán Duped the Brexiteers," *Spectator USA,* September 22, 2018, https://spectator.us/viktor-orban-duped-brexiteers/.

97 introduction to a short book: John O'Sullivan, *The Second Term of Viktor Orbán: Beyond Prejudice and Enthusiasm* (Social Affairs Unit, June 2015).

98 "neutral social structures": Christopher Caldwell, "Hungary and the Future of Europe: Viktor Orbán's Escalating Conflict with Liberalism," *Claremont Review of Books,* Spring 2019, https://claremontreviewofbooks.com/hungary-and-the-future -of-europe/.

100 "more favorable" to the Democratic Party: Author interview with John O'Sullivan, October 4, 2019.

102 "There is a legitimate question": Robert Merrick, "Fury as Boris Johnson Accuses Rebel Alliance MPs of 'Collabora-tion' with Foreign Governments over Brexit," *Independent,* October 1, 2019, https://www.independent.co.uk/news/uk /politics/boris-johnson-brexit-no-deal-latest-news-legal-advice -collusion-a9127781.html.

103 "After Brexit we also need": The Conservative and Unity Party Manifesto, 2019, https://assets-global.website-files.com /5da42e2cae7ebd3f8bde353c/5dda924905da587992a064ba _Conservative%202019%20Manifesto.pdf.

103 "misfits and weirdos": Rajeev Syal, "Dominic Cummings Calls for 'Weirdos and Misfits' for No 10 Jobs: Boris Johnson's Chief Adviser Touts for 'Unusual' Applicants Outside of the Oxbridge Set," *Guardian,* January 2, 2020, https://www .theguardian.com/politics/2020/jan/02/dominic-cummings -calls-for-weirdos-and-misfits-for-no-10-jobs.

104 "Great Britain has lost an empire but not yet found a role": Dean Acheson, speech at West Point, December 5, 1962.

IV *Cascades of Falsehood*

106 "authoritarian predisposition" she has identified: Author inter-view with Karen Stenner, July 19, 2019.

108 "capitalism is in deep trouble": Jean-François Revel, *The Totalitarian Temptation* (New York: Penguin Books, 1978).

109 "somewhere, in the past or in the future": Isaiah Berlin, *Four Essays on Liberty* (Oxford: Oxford University Press, 1992).

116 "Instead of hearing the harmony": Olga Tokarczuk, Nobel Prize Lecture, Swedish Academy, Stockholm, December 7, 2019, https://www.nobelprize.org/prizes/literature/2018 /tokarczuk/lecture/.

119 an advertisement for Vox: "Un nuevo comienzo," VOX, June 7, 2016, https://www.youtube.com/watch?v=RaSIX4-RPAI.

122 a "criminal organization": Ortega Smith, quoted in Anne Applebaum's "Want to Build a Far-Right Movement? Spain's VOX Party Shows How," *Washington Post,* May 2, 2019, https://www .washingtonpost.com/graphics/2019/opinions/spains-far-right-vox -party-shot-from-social-media-into-parliament-overnight-how/.

122 *#EspañaViva:* Santiago Abascal, Twitter post, https://twitter .com/Santi_ABASCAL/status/1062842722791424002?s=20.

123 "patriotic movement of salvation": Applebaum, "Want to Build a Far-Right Movement?"

124 "it was kind of a joke": Author interview with Rafael Bardaji.

127 "This was Spanish politics": Author interview with Ivan Espinosa, April 9, 2019.

134 4.5 million pro-Vox and anti-Islamic messages: Institute for Strategic Dialogue, *2019 EU Elections Information Operations Analysis: Interim Briefing Paper* (2019).

137 "hundreds of Muslims" were celebrating: Santiago Abascal, Twitter post, https://twitter.com/Santi_ABASCAL/status /1117890168340586497.

140 "We are trying to connect the past": Marion Maréchal, quoted in Anne Applebaum's "This Is How Reaganism and Thatcherism End," *Atlantic,* February 10, 2020, https://www .theatlantic.com/ideas/archive/2020/02/the-sad-path-from -reaganism-to-national-conservatism/606304/.

140 Macron himself was in Kraków: "Discours du Président Emmanuel Macron devant les étudiants de l'Université

Jagellonne de Cracovie," https://www.elysee.fr/emmanuel
-macron/2020/02/05/discours-du-president-emmanuel-macron
-devant-les-etudiants-de-luniversite-jagellonne-de-cracovie.

v *Prairie Fire*

143 "last, best hope of earth": Abraham Lincoln, Annual Message
to Congress, December 1, 1862.

144 "one day this nation will rise up": Rev. Martin Luther King Jr.,
"I Have a Dream" speech, Washington, DC, August 28, 1963.

144 "impressed from their cradle": Thomas Jefferson, letter to
John Breckinridge, January 29, 1800, https://founders.archives
.gov/documents/Jefferson/01-31-02-0292.

144 "shining city on a hill": Ronald Reagan, "Farewell Address to
the Nation," Washington, DC, January 12, 1989, https://www
.nytimes.com/1989/01/12/news/transcript-of-reagan-s-farewell
-address-to-american-people.html.

145 "A free Republic!": Emma Goldman, *Anarchism and Other
Essays* (New York: Mother Earth Pub. Association, 3rd rev.
edition, 1917).

145 "What is patriotism?": Emma Goldman, "What Is
Patriotism?," speech, April 26, 1908, San Francisco, California, https://awpc.cattcenter.iastate.edu/2017/03/09/what-is
-patriotism-april-26-1908/.

146 "modern martyrs who pay for their faith": Goldman, *Anarchism and Other Essays.*

147 "deadening ideology of conformism": *Prairie Fire: The Politics
of Revolutionary Anti-Imperialism—Political Statement of
the Weather Underground,* 1974, https://www.sds-1960s.org
/PrairieFire-reprint.pdf.

147 "myths of American exceptionalism": Howard Zinn, "The
Power and the Glory: The Myths of American Exceptionalism," *Boston Review,* June 1, 2005, http://bostonreview.net/zinn
-power-glory.

148 "A new and better age": Michael Gerson, "The Last Temptation," *Atlantic,* April 2018, https://www.theatlantic.com
/magazine/archive/2018/04/the-last-temptation/554066/.

149   "The only time we faced": Eric Metaxas, interview with Mike
      Gallagher, June 22, 2016, https://www.rightwingwatch.org/post
      /eric-metaxas-we-are-on-the-verge-of-losing-america-under
      -clinton-presidency-as-we-could-have-lost-it-in-the-civil-war/.

149   "I believe we are in the midnight hour": Brian Tashman,
      "Franklin Graham: 'The End Is Coming,' Thanks to Gays,
      Obama," *Right Wing Watch,* June 8, 2015, https://www
      .rightwingwatch.org/post/franklin-graham-the-end-is-coming
      -thanks-to-gays-obama/.

149   "popular culture that undergirded the values": Patrick J.
      Buchanan, official website, October 11, 1999, https://buchanan
      .org/blog/pjb-the-new-patriotism-329.

150   "In the popular culture of the '40s": Buchanan, official website,
      May 26, 2016, https://buchanan.org/blog/great-white-hope
      -125286.

150   "9/11 was a direct consequence": Patrick J. Buchanan, *Hard-
      ball,* September 30, 2002.

151   "multicultural, multiethnic, multiracial": Patrick J. Buchanan,
      "How to Avoid a New Cold War," *American Conservative,*
      January 3, 2017, https://www.theamericanconservative.com
      /buchanan/how-to-avoid-a-new-cold-war/.

152   "You know what solves": Donald Trump, interview, *Fox and
      Friends,* Fox News, February 10, 2014, https://video.foxnews
      .com/v/3179604851001#sp=show-clips.

152   "We're gonna have to have": Paul Blumenthal and
      J. M. Rieger, "Steve Bannon Thinks Dark Days Are Coming
      and War Is Inevitable," *Huffington Post,* February 8, 2017,
      https://www.huffpost.com/entry/steve-bannon-apocalypse_n
      _5898f02ee4b040613138a951.

153   quoting from the Bob Dylan song: Steve Bannon, speech,
      Tax Day Tea Party, New York, April 15, 2010, https://www
      .youtube.com/watch?v=Jf_Yj5XxUE0.

153   "Establishment" which had "protected itself": Donald J.
      Trump, inaugural address, Washington, DC, January 20,
      2017, https://www.whitehouse.gov/briefings-statements/the
      -inaugural-address/.

154   "The people, not the powerful": Donald J. Trump, "Remarks
      from President Trump to the People of Poland," Warsaw,
      July 6, 2017, https://www.whitehouse.gov/briefings-statements
      /remarks-president-trump-people-poland/.

155   "But he's a killer": Donald J. Trump, interview with Bill
      O'Reilly, Fox Sports, February 4, 2017, https://www.youtube
      .com/watch?v=tZXsYuJIGTg.

155   "He's running his country": Donald J. Trump, interview with
      Joe Scarborough, *Morning Joe,* December 18, 2015, https://
      www.washingtonpost.com/news/the-fix/wp/2015/12/18
      /donald-trump-glad-to-be-endorsed-by-russias-top-journalist
      -murderer/.

156   "Justice Department and White House–CIA types": *Prairie Fire.*

156   "You look at the corruption": Donald Trump, interview, *Fox
      and Friends,* Fox News, April 26, 2018, https://www.youtube
      .com/watch?v=5OjyHhz3_BM.

156   "To destroy a society": Jeane Kirkpatrick, "The Myth of
      Moral Equivalence," *Imprimis,* January 1986, https://imprimis
      .hillsdale.edu/the-myth-of-moral-equivalence/.

157   "America has no vital interest": Donald J. Trump and David
      Shiflett, *The America We Deserve* (New York: St. Martin's
      Press, 2000).

158   "It was cocktail hour": James Atlas, "The Counter Counter-
      culture," *New York Times Magazine,* February 12, 1995,
      https://www.nytimes.com/1995/02/12/magazine/the-counter
      -counterculture.html.

162   "intellectual intolerance and smug groupthink": David Brock,
      "Confessions of a Right-Wing Hit Man," *Esquire,* July 1, 1997,
      https://classic.esquire.com/confessions-of-a-right-wing-hit
      -man/.

162   I even wrote: "Why I Can't Vote for John McCain," Anne
      Applebaum, *Slate,* October 27, 2008.

162–3 "a cadre of the uprooted and displaced": Sam Tanenhaus,
      "On the Front Lines of the GOP's Civil War," *Esquire,*
      December 20, 2017, https://www.esquire.com/news-politics
      /a14428464/gop-never-trump/.

163 "when ethnic and nationalistic hatreds": Julien Benda, *The Treason of the Intellectuals,* trans. Richard Aldington (London: Taylor & Francis, 2017).

164 "disintegration of faith in reason": Roger Kimball, "The Treason of the Intellectuals & 'The Undoing of Thought,'" *New Criterion,* December 1992, https://newcriterion.com/issues /1992/12/the-treason-of-the-intellectuals-ldquothe-undoing-of -thoughtrdquo.

164 "angry mob which sided with Barabbas": Roger Kimball, *American Greatness,* November 2, 2019.

165 I was a guest on the program a couple of times: Anne Applebaum, *The Laura Ingraham Show,* August 19, 2008, http:// www.lauraingraham.com/b/Anne-Applebaum-on-the-return -of-the-Soviet-Union./5995.html.

166 "Is Western civilization": Laura Ingraham, interview with Patrick J. Buchanan, *The Laura Ingraham Show,* March 28, 2019, https://www.mediamatters.org/laura-ingraham/laura -ingraham-says-immigration-pushing-western-civilization -toward-tipping-over.

166 "the America that we know and love": Laura Ingraham, "The Left's Effort to Remake America," Fox News, August 8, 2018, https://www.youtube.com/watch?v=llhFZOw6Sss.

167 "it's going to be total war": Joseph diGenova, *The Laura Ingraham Podcast,* February 22, 2019.

167 "we don't want to be killed": Rafael Bardaji, quoted in Anne Applebaum, "Want to Build a Far-Right Movement? Spain's VOX Party Shows How," *Washington Post,* May 2, 2019, https://www.washingtonpost.com/graphics/2019/opinions/ spains-far-right-vox-party-shot-from-social-media-into -parliament-overnight-how/.

168 "a new pathway for hitting President Trump": Laura Ingraham, Fox News, February 25, 2020 https://twitter.com /MattGertz/status/1233026012201603079?s=20.

168 promoting the drug hydroxychloroquine: Michael M. Grynbaum, "Fox News Stars Trumpeted a Malaria Drug, Until They Didn't," *New York Times,* April 22, 2020.

168 "How many of those who urged our govt": Laura Ingraham, Twitter post, https://twitter.com/IngrahamAngle/status/1251219755249405959?s=20.

169 "without virtue there is no America": Laura Ingraham, "Laura Ingraham on Faith," speech, Dallas, Texas, September 29, 2007, https://www.youtube.com/watch?v=72KwL_abkOA.

170 "congratulations on your polling numbers": Laura Ingraham, interview with Donald Trump, Fox News, June 6, 2019, https://www.youtube.com/watch?v=QyQCcgXkANo.

171 "I was shouting from a tribune": Jacek Trznadel, *Hańba Domowa* (Paris: Instytut Literacki, 1986).

VI *The Unending of History*

173 "You are degrading an innocent man": Emile Zola, *The Dreyfus Affair: "J'Accuse" and Other Writings,* ed. Alain Pagès, trans. Eleanor Levieux (New Haven: Yale University Press, 1998).

173 "combat between two worlds": Romain Rolland, quoted in Tom Conner, *The Dreyfus Affair and the Rise of the French Public Intellectual* (Jefferson, NC: McFarland & Co., 2014).

174 "In every scientific work": Ferdinand Brunetière, *After the Trial,* quoted in Ruth Harris, *Dreyfus: Politics, Emotion, and the Scandal of the Century* (New York: Picador USA, 2010).

175 "J'accuse," published in 1898: Zola, *Dreyfus Affair.*

175 consider her "doubly meritorious": Marcel Proust, *Remembrance of Things Past,* trans. C. K. Scott Moncrieff (London: Penguin Classics, 2016).

176 "no less violent than the French Revolution or World War I": Quoted in Geert Mak, *In Europe: Travels Through the Twentieth Century* (London: Penguin Books, 2004), p. 10.

176 an ostentatiously "conservative outlook": Conner, *Dreyfus Affair.*

187 "Political regimes come and go": Ignazio Silone, "The Choice of Comrades," *Dissent,* Winter 1955, https://www.dissentmagazine.org/wp-content/files_mf/1438718063spring74silone.pdf.

ALSO BY

ANNE APPLEBAUM

RED FAMINE
Stalin's War on Ukraine

In 1929, Stalin launched agricultural collectivization—a policy that was, in effect, a second Russian revolution—which forced millions of peasants off their land and onto collective farms. The result was the most lethal famine in European history. Instead of sending relief, the Soviet state made use of the catastrophe to rid itself of a political problem. In *Red Famine*, Anne Applebaum argues that more than three million of those dead were Ukrainians who perished not because they were accidental victims of a bad policy but because the state deliberately set out to kill them. *Red Famine* captures the horror of ordinary people struggling to survive extraordinary evil. Applebaum's compulsively readable narrative recalls one of the worst crimes of the twentieth century and shows how it may foreshadow a new threat to the political order in the twenty-first.

History

BETWEEN EAST AND WEST
Across the Borderlands of Europe

Between East and West is an extraordinary journey into the past and present of the lands east of Poland and west of Russia—an area defined throughout its history by colliding empires. Traveling from the former Soviet naval center of Kaliningrad on the Baltic to the Black Sea port of Odessa, Anne Applebaum encounters a rich range of competing cultures, religions, and national aspirations. In reasserting their heritage, the inhabitants of the borderlands attempt to build a future grounded in their fractured ancestral legacies. *Between East and West* brilliantly illuminates the soul of the borderlands and the shaping power of the past.

History

IRON CURTAIN

The Crushing of Eastern Europe, 1944–1956

Anne Applebaum delivers a groundbreaking history of how Communism took over Eastern Europe after World War II and transformed in frightening fashion the individuals who came under its sway. *Iron Curtain* describes how, spurred by Stalin and his secret police, the Communist regimes of Eastern Europe were created and what daily life was like once they were complete. Drawing on newly opened East European archives, interviews, and personal accounts translated for the first time, Applebaum portrays in chilling detail the dilemmas faced by millions of individuals trying to adjust to a way of life that challenged their every belief and took away everything they had accumulated. As a result, the Soviet Bloc became a lost civilization, one whose cruelty, paranoia, bizarre morality, and strange aesthetics Applebaum captures in these electrifying pages.

History

GULAG

A History

Anne Applebaum offers the first fully documented portrait of the Gulag, from its origins in the Russian Revolution, through its expansion under Stalin, to its collapse in the era of glasnost. The Gulag—a vast array of Soviet concentration camps that held millions of political and criminal prisoners—was a system of repression and punishment that terrorized the entire society, embodying the worst tendencies of Soviet communism. Applebaum intimately re-creates what life was like in the camps and links them to the larger history of the Soviet Union.

History

ANCHOR BOOKS
Available wherever books are sold.
www.anchorbooks.com